ARCTIC OCEAN

Queen
Elizabeth
Islands

Ellesmere
Island

Greenland

East Siberian
Sea

Chukchi
Sea

Beaufort Sea

Banks
Island

Victoria
Island

Baffin

Davis Strait

Kolyma
Range

Brooks Range

Yukon

Mount McKinley
(Denali)
6194m

Mackenzie

Mackenzie
Mountains

Great Bear Lake

Great Slave Lake

Bay

Labrador
Sea

Kamchatka
Peninsula

Bering
Sea

Alaska Range

Gulf of
Alaska

Coast Mountains

ROCKY
Mountains

NORTH

Canadian Shield

AMERICA

Newfoundland

Aleutian Islands

Queen Charlotte
Islands

Vancouver Island

Lake
Winnipeg

Great Lakes

Nova Scotia

PACIFIC

OCEAN

Great
Basin

Great Plains

Missouri

Ohio

Appalachian Mts

ATLANTIC

OCEAN

Colorado

Mississippi

Midway
Islands

Hawaiian Islands

Rio Grande

Sierra Madre Occidental

Sierra Madre Oriental

Gulf of
Mexico

Bermuda

Bahamas

Hawaii

Cuba

Greater Antilles

West Indies

cronesia

Marshall Islands

line
nds

Melanesia

Tungaru

Line Islands

Polynesia

Caribbean
Sea

Lesser Antilles

Galapagos
Islands

Llanos

Orinoco

Guiana
Highlands

Marquesas
Islands

Amazon

Amazon
Basin

SOUTH

al
a

Solomon Islands

Vanuatu

Fiji

Samoa

Cook Islands

Tuamotu Islands

PACIFIC

AMERICA

New
Caledonia

Tonga

Austral
Islands

Pitcairn
Islands

OCEAN

Andes

Gran Chaco

Paraguay

Brazilian Highlands

Easter Island

Juan Fernandez
Islands

Cerro Aconcagua
6959m

Paraná

Uruguay

unt
ciuszko
28m

Tasman
Sea

North
Island

Pampas

nania

South
Island

New
Zealand

Chatham Islands

Patagonia

ATLANTIC

OCEAN

Falkland Islands

Tierra
del Fuego

Cape Horn

South Georgia

South Sandwich
Islands

SOUTHERN   OCEAN

Antarctic
Peninsula

Atlas
of the world

picthall and gunzi

picthall and gunzi

Created and produced by
Picthall & Gunzi Limited
21A Widmore Road
Bromley BR1 1RW
United Kingdom

Cartography:
Digital Cartography supplied by Encompass Graphics Ltd, Hove, U.K.

Cartographic Consultant: Roger Bullen

Editorial Direction: Christiane Gunzi
Senior Editor: Louise Pritchard
Editorial Assistant: Katy Rayner

Art Direction: Chez Picthall
Design: Gillian Shaw and Paul Calver
Picture Research: Gillian Shaw and Katy Rayner

Map Indexing: Roger Bullen and Paula Metcalf
General Indexer: Angie Hipkin

Production: Toby Reynolds

Written by: Chez Picthall
& Christiane Gunzi

ISBN 978 1 904618 82 9

Reproduction by Colourscan, Singapore
Printed and bound in Malaysia

Atlas
of the world

Chez Picthall

picthall and gunzi

Contents

North America

South America

Africa

Europe

Asia

Australasia and Oceania

The Arctic and Antarctica

All about maps

Maps show us what places on Earth look like from above. They give useful information, such as where towns and cities are, or where rivers and mountains run. A map can help us to find out where we are and can show us the distances between places. Maps have to carry a lot of information, so different symbols, lines and colours are used to show the features on the Earth's surface. Symbols are often used to show the position of towns, and lines show where all the country borders and rivers are.

A street map

A country map

Map scales Maps are 'large-' or 'small-' scale. Large-scale maps show small areas with lots of detail, like the street map above. Small-scale maps show large areas with less detail, like this country map. All the maps in this atlas are small-scale.

How maps are made

The most accurate world maps are globes because they are the same shape as planet Earth. To make a flat map out of a globe, map makers have to change the shape of Earth's surface. The land shapes get stretched and distorted. Map makers do this work mathematically, using what is called a 'projection'. There are many different kinds of projection, and each one looks slightly different. The people who create maps are called 'cartographers'.

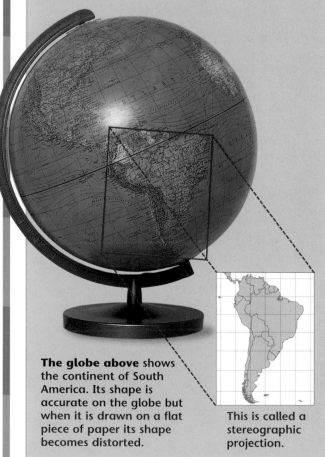
The globe above shows the continent of South America. Its shape is accurate on the globe but when it is drawn on a flat piece of paper its shape becomes distorted.

This is called a stereographic projection.

Latitude and longitude lines

To help us to locate places, we have invented invisible lines that run around the Earth. These are called the lines of latitude and longitude. Lines of latitude run horizontally. They measure how far north or south a place is from the Equator (around the Earth's middle). Longitude lines run from the North to the South Pole and measure how far east or west a place is from Greenwich, London. All these measurements are given in degrees and show a place's position on Earth.

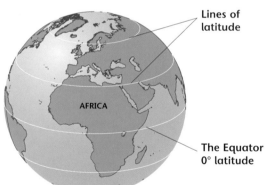
Lines of latitude

AFRICA

The Equator 0° latitude

Greenwich, London, UK 0° longitude

AFRICA

Lines of longitude

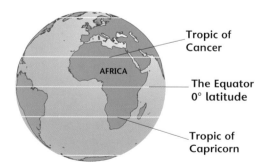
Tropic of Cancer

AFRICA

The Equator 0° latitude

Tropic of Capricorn

The Equator and the Tropics

The Equator is an imaginary line that runs around the centre of the Earth. It is an equal distance from the North and South Poles. Lying parallel to the Equator are lines called the Tropics of Cancer and Capricorn. Between these lines the climate and land are tropical.

North and South Poles

The North and South Poles are the most northerly and southerly points on the surface of the Earth. They are invisible and are found where all the lines of longitude meet. If you stood on the South Pole every direction would be north, and at the North Pole all directions would be south! There is no land at the North Pole, just the frozen waters of the Arctic Ocean.

North Pole

AFRICA

AFRICA

South Pole

How to use this atlas

The maps in this atlas have been arranged by continent in the following order: North America, South America, Africa, Europe, Asia, Australasia, Oceania and Antarctica. Every map has a double page and the countries on each map are listed at the top left-hand side for easy reference. Antarctica is shown with the Arctic, after all the other maps. Every map is accompanied by photographs of landscapes, wildlife, industries, famous landmarks, typical foods and interesting facts, to give you a snapshot of each area.

The indexes

This atlas has two indexes. One index gives a list of all the place names shown on the maps. The other index lists the animals, industries and other topics in the book. To find out how to use the indexes, see p.60.

Index to place names

Regional heading tells you which region or country the map shows.

Continent heading tells you which continent the region is in.

Introductory text sets the scene for each map, giving general information about the region.

Did you know? boxes give you some fascinating facts about the countries on each of the maps.

Locator globe shows you which region of the world the map covers.

Country File lists all the countries shown on the map.

Photographs of animals, people and places help to bring the map to life.

Compass rose shows the direction of north for each map.

Grid letters and numbers help you to find the cities, towns, rivers, mountains and other features listed in the index to the place names.

Flags of each nation are shown next to their country.

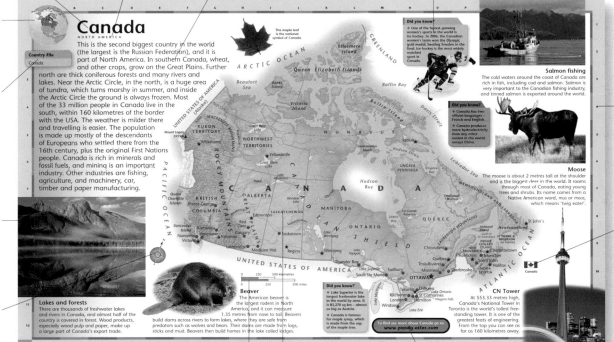

Scale bar helps you to work out the distances between places and how big countries are.

Map colours show you how high the land is.

Find out more directs you to a website where you can find more information about topics featured on the page.

Key to all the features on the maps:

Land height

2,000 metres

1,000 metres

500 metres

200 metres

Sea level

Map features

Grand Canyon	Physical feature	*Great Salt Lake*	Salt lake	★SUCRE	Capital city
▲*Kilimanjaro*	Mountain height	*Dodecanese*	Island group	Cali ●	Major city
Limpopo	River	*Cape of Good Hope*	Headland	★ Helena	State capital
Angel Falls	Waterfall	*Beaufort Sea*	Sea	ALBANIA	Country
Lake Okeechobee	Lake	*ATLANTIC OCEAN*	Ocean	MARTINIQUE (to France)	Dependent territory

IOWA	State
	Country border
	State border
	Disputed border

Our planet in space

If we wrote down the address for planet Earth it would be: The Earth, The Solar System, The Milky Way, The Universe. Our Earth belongs to the Solar System, which forms just a tiny part of the Milky Way galaxy. A galaxy is a massive group of hundreds of billions of stars. The Milky Way is one of billions of galaxies in the Universe. The Universe is the name that we give to the whole of space.

The Milky Way

Our Sun is one of 200 billion stars in the Milky Way. The Milky Way is a spiral galaxy and it is really enormous. It would take 100,000 'light years' to travel across it!

The Solar System

Our Solar System is made up of the Sun and the eight planets and other bodies (such as comets, moons and asteroids) that orbit around it. The Sun is a star. Its powerful gravity keeps everything orbiting around it. The four planets that are nearest to the Sun (Mercury, Venus, Earth and Mars) are made of rock and metal. The four outer planets (Jupiter, Saturn, Uranus and Neptune) are mostly gas or liquid. They are known as 'the gas giants'.

Pluto

Pluto used to be called a planet. But in 2006 the International Astronomical Union decided that it is only a 'dwarf planet'.

Neptune

This is the furthest planet from the Sun. A French mathematician discovered its existence in 1843 by doing calculations, but it was not actually seen for another three years.

Uranus

The blue colour of Uranus comes from the gas called methane, which is in its atmosphere. Scientists think that this planet is made of different icy materials (methane, water and ammonia) surrounding a solid core.

Saturn

This planet is surrounded by many 'rings'. These rings are a few hundred metres thick and about 270,000 kilometres in diameter. They are formed from millions of icy particles. The ice particles range in size from tiny pieces a few millimetres across to huge lumps that are tens of metres across.

Did you know?

◈ Distances in space are so huge that scientists measure them in 'light years'. A light year is the distance that light travels in one year, which is 9,460 billion kilometres!

◈ The light coming from the Sun takes a little over eight minutes to reach Earth.

The relative distance of the planets from the Sun

Neptune
This is about 4.5 billion km from the Sun.

Uranus

Saturn

Jupiter

Sun

Venus

Earth

Mars

Mercury

The Sun

The Sun is about 4.5 billion years old and is only half-way through its life. It is 1.4 million kilometres across and is made mostly of the gases hydrogen and helium. The temperature at its surface is 5,500°C.

The Moon

Earth's Moon has no water and is made of solid rock. It is covered in craters made by meteorites that crashed into it.

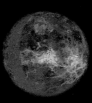

Mercury

The planet that is closest to the Sun is Mercury. This means that it has the shortest year (the time that it takes to go once round the Sun) of all the planets.

Venus

The planet Venus is the brightest object in our night sky, after the Moon. This is because its atmosphere reflects more sunlight than any other planet.

Earth

The Earth is the third planet from the Sun and, as far as we know, it is the only planet in our Solar System that has any kind of life on it.

Mars

Bright red dust covers most of the planet Mars. The dust often blows into fierce sandstorms. When this happens, the surface of the planet cannot be seen.

Did you know?

To qualify as a planet, a body must:
1) Orbit around a sun.
2) Be big enough for its own gravity to have pulled it into a ball.
3) Have cleared other bodies out of its orbit.

Pluto does not qualify on the third point, so in 2006 it was downgraded from a planet to a 'dwarf planet'.

Jupiter

This giant planet is made almost entirely of gas. Jupiter is the largest planet in the Solar System and it is 11 times larger in diameter than Earth.

Planet Earth's many layers

The rocky layer of Earth that we live on is called the crust. It is about 40 kilometres thick. Scientists believe that the inner core of Earth is solid iron. This is surrounded by a molten layer of iron and nickel, which is called the outer core. Between the Earth's outer core and its crust is the mantle.

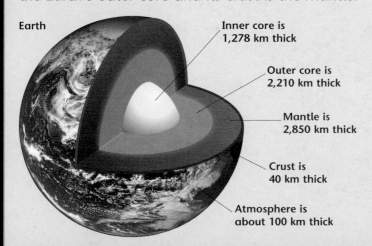

Earth

Inner core is 1,278 km thick

Outer core is 2,210 km thick

Mantle is 2,850 km thick

Crust is 40 km thick

Atmosphere is about 100 km thick

When the surface of the Earth moves

The Earth's crust is made up of 'tectonic plates', which are constantly moving and pushing past each other. Most of the time the movements are so small that we do not notice them. But sometimes, during an earthquake or a volcanic eruption, the Earth moves violently and these movements are easy to notice.

Earthquake

When tectonic plates 'stick' together instead of sliding past each other, stress builds up in the rocks until they crack or 'fault'. This cracking sends shock waves through the Earth, causing an earthquake. Powerful earthquakes can sometimes destroy whole cities.

Volcano

Where the Earth's crust is weak, or at the point between two tectonic plates, magma (molten rock) seeps out and volcanoes can develop over time. The pressure of magma pushing up to the Earth's surface can be so powerful that a volcano will erupt, spewing out lava.

Physical features of the world

Greenland · Greenland Sea · Spitsbergen · Franz Josef Land · Severnaya Zemlya · New Siberian Islands

Novaya Zemlya · Kara Sea · Taymyr Peninsula · Laptev Sea

Barents Sea · North Siberian Lowland · Central Siberian Plateau

Arctic Circle · Denmark Strait · Norwegian Sea · Pechora · Ob' · West Siberian Plain · Siberia · Verkhoyanskiy Khrebet

Iceland · Lake Onega · Yenisey · Lena

Faeroe Islands · Northern Dvina · Ob' · Angara · Lena · Aldan

Lake Ladoga · Ural Mountains · Yenisey · Lake Baikal · Sea of Okhotsk

North Sea · North European Plain · Volga · Irtysh · ASIA · Amur · Sakh...

Ireland · Britain · Baltic Sea · EUROPE · Lake Balkhash · Altai Mountains · Manchurian Plain

ATLANTIC · Bay of Biscay · Alps · Carpathian Mountains · Dnieper · Don · Volga · Aral Sea · Tien Shan · Takla Makan Desert · Gobi · Sea of Japan · Hok...

OCEAN · Loire · Rhine · Danube · Black Sea · Caspian Sea · Amu Darya · Yellow River · Great Plain of China · Yellow Sea · Honsh...

Azores · Iberian Peninsula · Mediterranean Sea · Anatolia · Caucasus · ▲El'brus 5642m · Euphrates · Tigris · Zagros Mountains · Iranian Plateau · Hindu Kush · Plateau of Tibet · Shikoku · Kyushu

Atlas Mountains · The Gulf · Himalayas · Brahmaputra · Yangtze · East China Sea

Canary Islands · Libyan Desert · Nile · Red Sea · Arabian Peninsula · Indus · Thar Desert · Ganges · ▲Mount Everest 8850m · Irrawaddy · Xi Jiang · Taiwan

Tropic of Cancer · Sahara Desert · Arabian Sea · Deccan · Salween · Philippine Sea · Mariana Islands

Cape Verde Islands · Senegal · Niger · Sahel · Lake Chad · White Nile · Blue Nile · Gulf of Aden · Laccadive Islands · Bay of Bengal · Mekong · South China Sea · Phillipine Islands · Mi...

AFRICA · Ethiopian Highlands · Andaman Islands · Malay Peninsula · Car... Isle...

Equator · Gulf of Guinea · Ubangi · Great Rift Valley · Maldive Islands · Nicobar Islands · Sri Lanka · Celebes Sea · East Indies · New Guinea

Ascension Island · Congo · Congo Basin · Lake Victoria · ▲Kilimanjaro 5895m · Seychelles · Chagos Archipelago · Sumatra · Borneo · Java Sea · Sulawesi

St Helena · Great Rift Valley · Lake Tanganyika · Lake Nyasa · Comoros Islands · Cocos Islands · Java · Timor · Arafura Sea

Namib Desert · Zambezi · Mozambique Channel · Madagascar · Mauritius · Réunion · INDIAN · Great Di...

Tropic of Capricorn · Kalahari Desert · OCEAN · Great Sandy Desert · Simpson Desert

ATLANTIC · Orange River · AUSTRALIA

OCEAN · Cape of Good Hope · Nullarbor Plain · Darling

Great Australian Bight · ▲Mount Kosciuszko 2228m

Prince Edward Islands · Crozet Islands · Tasmania

Kerguelen

Antarctic Circle · SOUTHERN OCEAN

ANTARCTICA

10

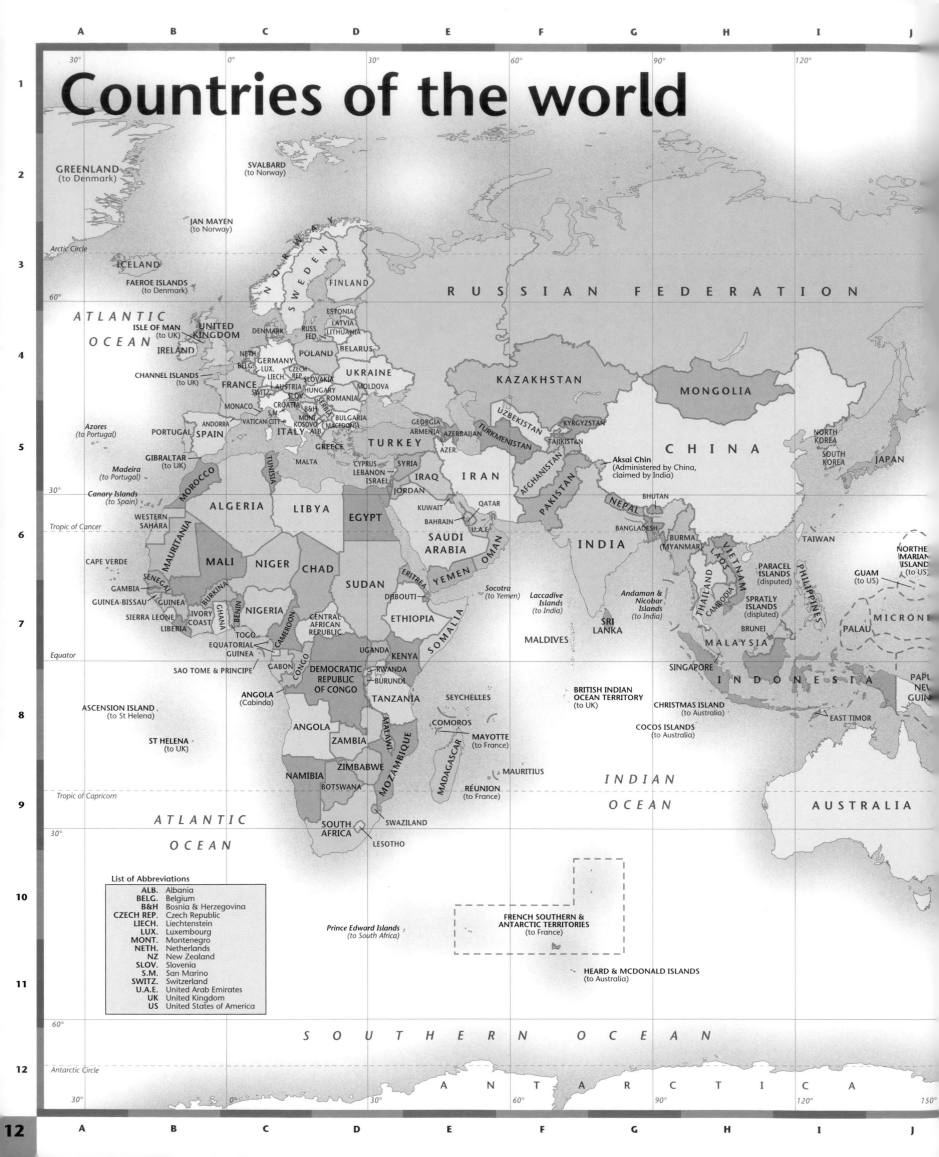

Countries of the world

GREENLAND
(to Denmark)

SVALBARD
(to Norway)

JAN MAYEN
(to Norway)

Arctic Circle

ICELAND

FAEROE ISLANDS
(to Denmark)

60°

ATLANTIC

OCEAN

ISLE OF MAN
(to UK)

UNITED
KINGDOM

IRELAND

CHANNEL ISLANDS
(to UK)

NORWAY

SWEDEN

FINLAND

ESTONIA
LATVIA
LITHUANIA

DENMARK
RUSS.
FED.

BELARUS

NETH.
BELG.
LUX.
GERMANY
CZECH
REP.
LIECH.
SLOV.
SWITZ.
AUSTRIA HUNGARY
MONACO
S.M.
CROATIA
B&H
SERBIA
MONT.
KOSOVO
MACEDONIA
ALB.

POLAND

UKRAINE

MOLDOVA

ROMANIA

BULGARIA

RUSSIAN FEDERATION

KAZAKHSTAN

MONGOLIA

NORTH
KOREA
SOUTH
KOREA

JAPAN

FRANCE

Azores
(to Portugal)

ANDORRA
PORTUGAL SPAIN

VATICAN CITY
ITALY

GREECE

MALTA

GEORGIA
ARMENIA
AZERBAIJAN
AZER.

TURKMENISTAN

UZBEKISTAN

KYRGYZSTAN

TAJIKISTAN

CHINA

Madeira
(to Portugal)

GIBRALTAR
(to UK)

MOROCCO

TUNISIA

CYPRUS
LEBANON
ISRAEL
SYRIA

TURKEY

IRAQ

IRAN

AFGHANISTAN

Aksai Chin
(Administered by China,
claimed by India)

Canary Islands
(to Spain)

30°

WESTERN
SAHARA

ALGERIA

LIBYA

EGYPT

JORDAN

KUWAIT
BAHRAIN

QATAR
U.A.E.

PAKISTAN

NEPAL

BHUTAN

Tropic of Cancer

MAURITANIA

CAPE VERDE

MALI

NIGER

CHAD

SAUDI
ARABIA

OMAN

BANGLADESH

INDIA

BURMA
(MYANMAR)

TAIWAN

NORTHE
MARIAN
ISLAND
(to US

GUAM
(to US)

SENEGAL
GAMBIA
GUINEA-BISSAU
GUINEA
SIERRA LEONE
LIBERIA
IVORY
COAST
BURKINA
GHANA
BENIN
TOGO

NIGERIA

SUDAN

ERITREA

YEMEN

DJIBOUTI

Socotra
(to Yemen)

Laccadive
Islands
(to India)

Andaman &
Nicobar
Islands
(to India)

THAILAND
LAOS
VIETNAM
CAMBODIA

PARACEL
ISLANDS
(disputed)

PHILIPPINES

MICRONE

Equator

CAMEROON
EQUATORIAL
GUINEA
SAO TOME & PRINCIPE
GABON
CONGO

CENTRAL
AFRICAN
REPUBLIC

ETHIOPIA

SOMALIA

UGANDA
KENYA

DEMOCRATIC
REPUBLIC
OF CONGO

RWANDA
BURUNDI

MALDIVES

SRI
LANKA

SPRATLY
ISLANDS
(disputed)

BRUNEI

MALAYSIA

PALAU

PAPU
NEV
GUIN

SINGAPORE

INDONESIA

ANGOLA
(Cabinda)

TANZANIA

SEYCHELLES

BRITISH INDIAN
OCEAN TERRITORY
(to UK)

CHRISTMAS ISLAND
(to Australia)

COCOS ISLANDS
(to Australia)

EAST TIMOR

ASCENSION ISLAND
(to St Helena)

ANGOLA

ZAMBIA

MALAWI

MOZAMBIQUE

COMOROS

MAYOTTE
(to France)

ST HELENA
(to UK)

NAMIBIA

ZIMBABWE

BOTSWANA

MADAGASCAR

Réunion
(to France)

MAURITIUS

INDIAN

OCEAN

AUSTRALIA

Tropic of Capricorn

ATLANTIC

OCEAN

SOUTH
AFRICA

SWAZILAND

LESOTHO

30°

List of Abbreviations

ALB.	Albania
BELG.	Belgium
B&H	Bosnia & Herzegovina
CZECH REP.	Czech Republic
LIECH.	Liechtenstein
LUX.	Luxembourg
MONT.	Montenegro
NETH.	Netherlands
NZ	New Zealand
SLOV.	Slovenia
S.M.	San Marino
SWITZ.	Switzerland
U.A.E.	United Arab Emirates
UK	United Kingdom
US	United States of America

Prince Edward Islands
(to South Africa)

FRENCH SOUTHERN &
ANTARCTIC TERRITORIES
(to France)

HEARD & MCDONALD ISLANDS
(to Australia)

60°

SOUTHERN   OCEAN

Antarctic Circle

ANTARCTICA

30°

12

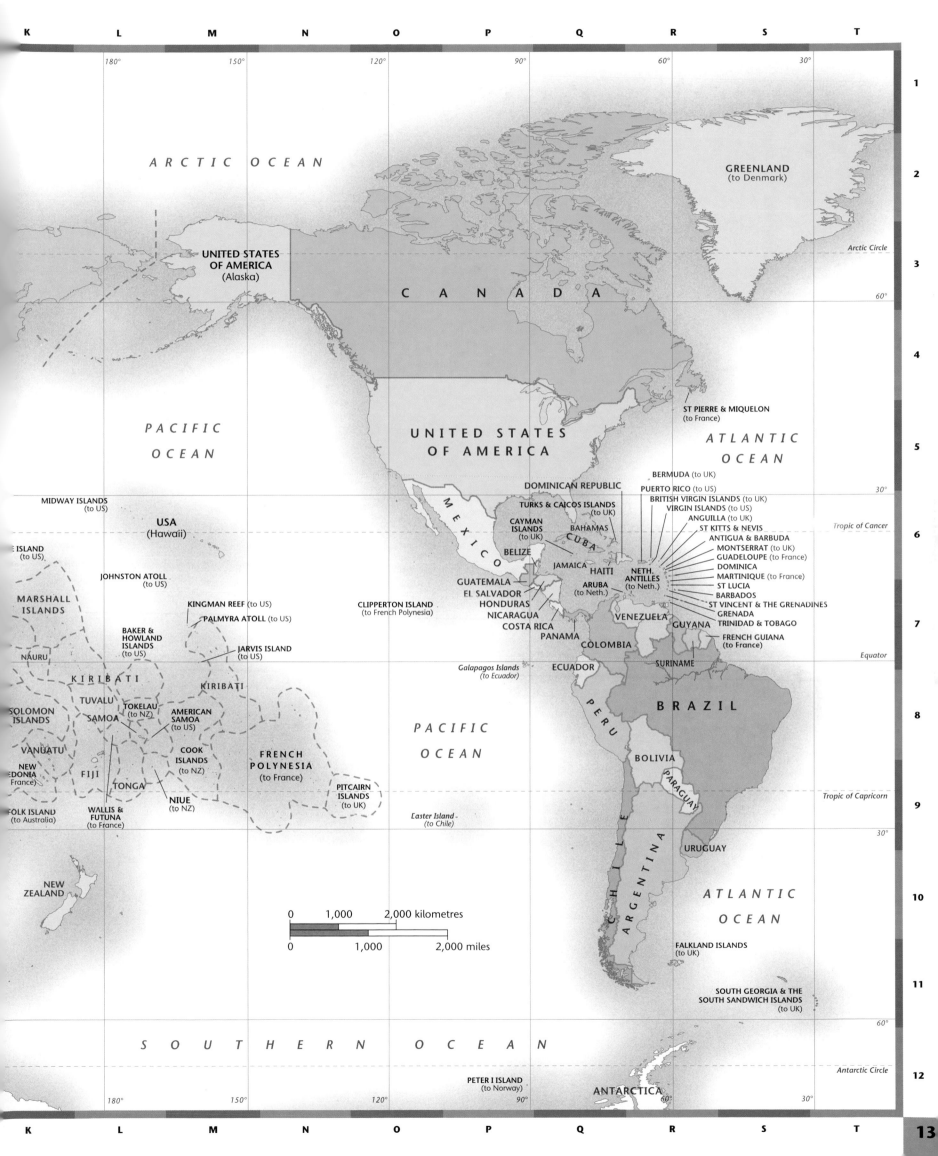

180° 150° 120° 90° 60° 30°

1

ARCTIC OCEAN

GREENLAND
(to Denmark)

2

Arctic Circle

3

UNITED STATES
OF AMERICA
(Alaska)

C A N A D A

60°

4

PACIFIC

OCEAN

ST PIERRE & MIQUELON
(to France)

ATLANTIC

OCEAN

5

UNITED STATES
OF AMERICA

BERMUDA (to UK)

PUERTO RICO (to US)

30°

DOMINICAN REPUBLIC

BRITISH VIRGIN ISLANDS (to UK)

MIDWAY ISLANDS
(to US)

TURKS & CAICOS ISLANDS
(to UK)

VIRGIN ISLANDS (to US)

ANGUILLA (to UK)

USA
(Hawaii)

CAYMAN
ISLANDS
(to UK)

BAHAMAS

ST KITTS & NEVIS

Tropic of Cancer

6

MEXICO

CUBA

ANTIGUA & BARBUDA

E ISLAND
(to US)

BELIZE

MONTSERRAT (to UK)

GUADELOUPE (to France)

JOHNSTON ATOLL
(to US)

JAMAICA

HAITI

NETH.
ANTILLES
(to Neth.)

DOMINICA

MARTINIQUE (to France)

MARSHALL
ISLANDS

KINGMAN REEF (to US)

GUATEMALA

ARUBA
(to Neth.)

ST LUCIA

BARBADOS

PALMYRA ATOLL (to US)

EL SALVADOR

HONDURAS

ST VINCENT & THE GRENADINES

BAKER &
HOWLAND
ISLANDS
(to US)

CLIPPERTON ISLAND
(to French Polynesia)

NICARAGUA

GRENADA

NAURU

JARVIS ISLAND
(to US)

COSTA RICA

PANAMA

VENEZUELA

GUYANA

TRINIDAD & TOBAGO

FRENCH GUIANA
(to France)

7

COLOMBIA

Galapagos Islands
(to Ecuador)

ECUADOR

SURINAME

Equator

KIRIBATI

KIRIBATI

PERU

BRAZIL

8

TUVALU

SOLOMON
ISLANDS

TOKELAU
(to NZ)

SAMOA

AMERICAN
SAMOA
(to US)

PACIFIC

OCEAN

VANUATU

COOK
ISLANDS
(to NZ)

FRENCH
POLYNESIA
(to France)

BOLIVIA

NEW
EDONIA
France)

FIJI

TONGA

NIUE
(to NZ)

PARAGUAY

Tropic of Capricorn

9

FOLK ISLAND
(to Australia)

WALLIS &
FUTUNA
(to France)

PITCAIRN
ISLANDS
(to UK)

Easter Island
(to Chile)

CHILE

ARGENTINA

URUGUAY

30°

NEW
ZEALAND

0 1,000 2,000 kilometres

ATLANTIC

OCEAN

10

0 1,000 2,000 miles

FALKLAND ISLANDS
(to UK)

11

SOUTH GEORGIA & THE
SOUTH SANDWICH ISLANDS
(to UK)

S O U T H E R N   O C E A N

60°

12

Antarctic Circle

PETER I ISLAND
(to Norway)

ANTARCTICA

180° 150° 120° 90° 60° 30°

Climate and land cover

Climate is the average pattern of the weather over about 30 years. The climate of a place depends on how much sunshine and rain it gets, how close it is to the sea and sea currents, and how high it is above sea level. Different kinds of plants grow in different climates. The type of vegetation in an area, such as grassland or tropical forest, is called 'land cover'. Different land cover is suitable for different animals. The countries around the Equator get the most sunlight and rain. It is there that the habitats with the largest numbers of animals and plants are found. In places where there is little rainfall or the temperatures are too hot or cold, such as the Sahara or the North and South Poles, only a few species of plants and animals are able to survive.

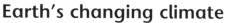

Temperate broadleaf forest

Forests in temperate parts of the world have mild temperatures and plenty of rain. These forests contain trees such as oak, beech, birch and chestnut. Broadleaved trees collect nutrients in summer and shed their leaves in autumn to save energy and water.

Tropical broadleaf forest

Tropical forests that grow near the Equator have high temperatures and receive heavy rainfall all year round. These forests may contain over 50,000 different species of trees, as well as huge numbers of other plants and animals.

Earth's changing climate

The world's climate is gradually changing, and this is having huge effects on its wildlife and people. Some areas have unusual floods and other places are affected by drought. Many kinds of animals, including polar bears, are threatened by climate change. Not all the animals and plants will be able to adapt to these new conditions. In the most badly affected areas some species will die out.

Extreme weather

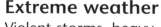

Violent storms, heavy rainfall, strong winds and long periods of sunshine are all examples of extreme weather. Extreme weather often causes widespread flooding or drought, and the effects of these can be devastating. People may be killed or left homeless, and crops, farm animals and wildlife may be destroyed.

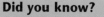

▪ Needleleaf forest

Stretching across northern parts of Asia, Europe and North America is a belt of tall, evergreen trees with needle-like leaves. They can survive cold winters because they gather nutrients all year.

▪ Cropland

Many of the most fertile areas of the world, especially Europe and North America, do not have their natural land cover. This has been cleared over hundreds of years to grow crops for food.

▪ Grassland

In areas of a continent where there is not enough rain for trees to grow, there are huge grasslands. These are called steppes and prairies in the north. In South America they are known as pampas.

▪ Tundra

Areas of tundra are mostly found near the Arctic Circle. The soil is frozen for much of the year. In places where it melts for a few months, plants such as lichens, mosses and low shrubs are able to grow.

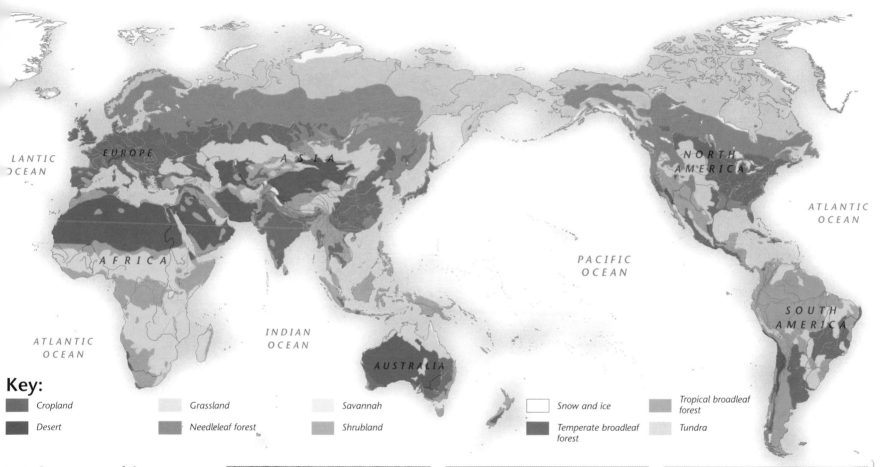

Key:

- ▪ Cropland
- ▪ Desert
- ▪ Grassland
- ▪ Needleleaf forest
- ▪ Savannah
- ▪ Shrubland
- ▪ Snow and ice
- ▪ Temperate broadleaf forest
- ▪ Tropical broadleaf forest
- ▪ Tundra

▪ Snow and ice

In the Arctic and Antarctica, and on the highest parts of mountain ranges, such as the Alps and the Andes, there is snow and ice all year round. Temperatures remain well below freezing and it is often windy. Very few animals and plants can survive in such a harsh environment.

▪ Shrubland

At the edges of both hot and cold deserts there are areas of shrubland. Where it is too hot or too cold for trees to survive, tough, spiny shrubs with small leaves grow well.

▪ Desert

Deserts have very little water and are often windy. Few plants or animals can survive, as temperatures soar to over 40°C in the day and drop to below freezing at night.

▪ Savannah

Between hot deserts and tropical forests are areas called savannah. There is grass here and lots of trees, but the trees do not grow close together in big groups.

Planet Earth's population

Every second, the world's population gets larger by two or three people. About 100 years ago, there were 1,625 million people on Earth, but by 2010 there may be more than 6,900 million. Scientists have worked out that the world's population will reach 9,000 million in 2050, at today's rates of births and deaths. People live in most parts of the world, but they are not evenly distributed. Some countries, such as Singapore, have dense populations with thousands of people for every square kilometre of land (which is called its population density), but others, such as Mongolia, have fewer than two people for every square kilometre. Most of the areas where hardly any people live are either too hot and dry, such as the Sahara, or too cold, such as the poles.

Is there enough for everyone?

As the world's population continues to grow bigger, more houses, food, water and fuel are needed. In some areas there is not enough clean water or shelter for everyone. Some countries cannot grow enough food, and do not have enough fuel supplies.

World population

This map shows how the world's population is spread out. Most people live in South and East Asia. In 1900 only a few towns had more than 1 million people living in them. Now 25 of the world's cities have over 15 million people.

EUROPE has mostly warm summers and mild winters, and much of the land is fertile and easy to farm, which provides ideal living conditions.

AFRICA has the Sahara, which is the biggest desert in the world. Living here is difficult because the temperatures range from 50°C during the day to below 0°C at night. Most people living here belong to nomadic tribes.

SOUTH ASIA has the biggest, and one of the fastest-growing populations in the world. One-fifth of the world's population lives in this area.

ATLANTIC OCEAN

RUSSIAN FEDERATION

ASIA

AFRICA

INDIAN OCEAN

AUSTRALIA

Cairo

Karachi

Delhi

Mumbai

Kolkata

Seoul

Tokyo

Osaka

Shanghai

Manila

Jakarta

Busy, busy cities

In the 1900s, only 1 out of every 10 people lived in a city. Now more than 5 out of 10 people live in cities. India and China have the most cities with over one million people, even though two-thirds of their populations live in the countryside. By 2030 almost two-thirds of the world's population may live in cities.

Population growth

The world's population is now more than six times bigger than it was 200 years ago. This is mostly due to better healthcare and improved ways of growing food and supplying clean water. A well-fed population with better healthcare means that more babies are being born alive and more of them survive, and people are living longer too.

These are the most populated countries in the world.

In 2007 there were 11 countries with national populations of more than 100,000,000 people.

1	China	1,321,851,888
2	India	1,129,866,154
3	USA	301,139,947
4	Indonesia	234,693,997
5	Brazil	190,010.647
6	Pakistan	164,741,924
7	Bangladesh	150,448,339
8	Russia	141,377,752
9	Nigeria	135,031,164
10	Japan	127,433,494
11	Mexico	108,700,891

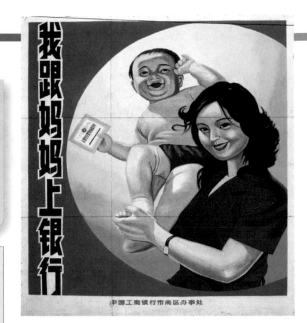

Controlling the population

In some parts of the world people have large families. This can be because of religious beliefs, traditions or due to poverty. To help slow down population growth, many governments now teach people how to plan their families better. In China the government has ruled that couples may not have more than one child without permission.

Key to the map:

People per square kilometre

- More than 1,000
- 100–999
- 50–99
- 10–49
- 1–9
- Less than 1

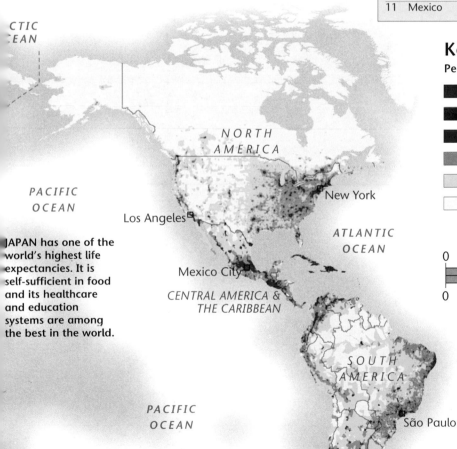

NORTH AMERICA

New York

Los Angeles

PACIFIC OCEAN

JAPAN has one of the world's highest life expectancies. It is self-sufficient in food and its healthcare and education systems are among the best in the world.

Mexico City

ATLANTIC OCEAN

CENTRAL AMERICA & THE CARIBBEAN

SOUTH AMERICA

PACIFIC OCEAN

São Paulo

0 ——— 2,000 kilometres

0 ——— 2,000 miles

ARCTIC OCEAN

SOUTH AMERICA has a population that is mainly around the coast and in the northern parts of the Andes. The population in many towns has grown enormously because people have moved from the countryside to the towns to find work.

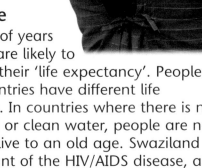

How long people live

The number of years that people are likely to live is called their 'life expectancy'. People in different countries have different life expectancies. In countries where there is not enough food or clean water, people are not expected to live to an old age. Swaziland has a high amount of the HIV/AIDS disease, and life expectancy is 32 years. Japan is one of the richest countries and has one of the highest life expectancies, at about 82 years. The country with the highest is Andorra, at over 83 years.

Flags and facts

All the countries in the world have their own national flag. Flags are colourful symbols of their country's people and government. The population of every country changes daily. Most countries have a growing population, but some populations decrease due to war, natural disasters or political pressure. Below is a list of all the continents and countries. Each country's flag, capital city and population are included.

NORTH AMERICA
Canada p.20

Canada
Capital City Ottawa
Population 33,390,141

USA p.22

United States of America
Capital City Washington DC
Population 301,139,947

Central America and the Caribbean p.24

Antigua and Barbuda
Capital City St John's
Population 69,481

Bahamas
Capital City Nassau
Population 305,655

Barbados
Capital City Bridgetown
Population 280,946

Belize
Capital City Belmopan
Population 294,385

Costa Rica
Capital City San Jose
Population 4,133,884

Cuba
Capital City Havana
Population 11,394,043

Dominica
Capital City Roseau
Population 72,386

Dominican Republic
Capital City Santo Domingo
Population 9,365,818

El Salvador
Capital City San Salvador
Population 6,948,073

Grenada
Capital City St George's
Population 89,971

Guatemala
Capital City Guatemala City
Population 12,728,111

Haiti
Capital City Port-au-Prince
Population 8,706,497

Honduras
Capital City Tegucigalpa
Population 7,483,763

Jamaica
Capital City Kingston
Population 2,780,132

Mexico
Capital City Mexico City
Population 108,700,891

Nicaragua
Capital City Managua
Population 5,675,356

Panama
Capital City Panama City
Population 3,242,173

St Lucia
Capital City Castries
Population 170,649

St Kitts and Nevis
Capital City Basseterre
Population 39,349

St Vincent and the Grenadines
Capital City Kingstown
Population 118,149

Trinidad and Tobago
Capital City Port-of-Spain
Population 1,056,608

SOUTH AMERICA
South America p.26

Argentina
Capital City Buenos Aires
Population 40,301,927

Bolivia
Capital Cities La Paz and Sucre
Population 9,119,152

Brazil
Capital City Brasilia
Population 190,010,647

Chile
Capital City Santiago
Population 16,284,741

Colombia
Capital City Bogota
Population 44,379,598

Ecuador
Capital City Quito
Population 13,755,680

Guyana
Capital City Georgetown
Population 769,095

Paraguay
Capital City Asuncion
Population 6,669,086

Peru
Capital City Lima
Population 28,674,757

Suriname
Capital City Paramaribo
Population 470,784

Uruguay
Capital City Montevideo
Population 3,460,607

Venezuela
Capital City Caracas
Population 26,023,528

AFRICA
Northern Africa p.28

Algeria
Capital City Algiers
Population 33,333,216

Benin
Capital City Porto-Novo
Population 8,078,314

Burkina Faso
Capital City Ouagadougou
Population 14,326,203

Cameroon
Capital City Yaounde
Population 18,060,382

Cape Verde
Capital City Praia
Population 423,613

Central African Republic
Capital City Bangui
Population 4,369,038

Chad
Capital City Ndjamena
Population 9,885,661

Djibouti
Capital City Djibouti
Population 496,374

Egypt
Capital City Cairo
Population 80,335,036

Eritrea
Capital City Asmara
Population 4,906,585

Ethiopia
Capital City Addis Ababa
Population 76,511,887

Gambia
Capital City Banjul
Population 1,688,359

Ghana
Capital City Accra
Population 22,931,299

Guinea
Capital City Conakry
Population 9,947,814

Guinea-Bissau
Capital City Bissau
Population 1,472,780

Ivory Coast
Capital City Yamoussoukro
Population 18,013,409

Liberia
Capital City Monrovia
Population 3,195,931

Libya
Capital City Tripoli
Population 6,036,914

Mali
Capital City Bamako
Population 11,995,402

Mauritania
Capital City Nouakchott
Population 3,270,065

Morocco
Capital City Rabat
Population 33,757,175

Niger
Capital City Niamey
Population 12,894,865

Nigeria
Capital City Abuja
Population 135,031,164

Senegal
Capital City Dakar
Population 12,521,851

Sierra Leone
Capital City Freetown
Population 6,144,562

Somalia
Capital City Mogadishu
Population 9,118,773

Sudan
Capital City Khartoum
Population 39,379,358

Togo
Capital City Lome
Population 5,701,579

Tunisia
Capital City Tunis
Population 10,276,158

Western Sahara
Capital City Laayoune
Population 382,617

Southern Africa p.30

Angola
Capital City Luanda
Population 12,263,596

Botswana
Capital City Gaborone
Population 1,815,508

Burundi
Capital City Bujumbura
Population 8,390,505

Comoros
Capital City Moroni
Population 711,417

Congo
Capital City Brazzaville
Population 3,800,610

Congo, DR
Capital City Kinshasa
Population 65,751,512

Equatorial Guinea
Capital City Malabo
Population 551,201

Gabon
Capital City Libreville
Population 1,454,867

Kenya
Capital City Nairobi
Population 36,913,721

Lesotho
Capital City Maseru
Population 2,125,262

Madagascar
Capital City Antananarivo
Population 19,448,815

Malawi
Capital City Lilongwe
Population 13,603,181

Mauritius
Capital City Port Louis
Population 1,250,882

Mozambique
Capital City Maputo
Population 20,905,585

Namibia
Capital City Windhoek
Population 2,055,080

Rwanda
Capital City Kigali
Population 9,907,509

Sao Tome and Principe
Capital City Sao Tome
Population 199,579

Seychelles
Capital City Victoria
Population 81,895

South Africa
Capital Cities Bloemfontein, Cape Town and Tshwane (Pretoria)
Population 43,997,828

Swaziland
Capital City Mbabane
Population 1,133,066

Tanzania
Capital City Dodoma
Population 39,384,223

Uganda
Capital City Kampala
Population 30,262,610

Zambia
Capital City Lusaka
Population 11,477,447

Zimbabwe
Capital City Harare
Population 12,311,143

EUROPE
Northern Europe p.32

Denmark
Capital City Copenhagen
Population 5,468,120

Estonia
Capital City Tallinn
Population 1,315,912

Finland
Capital City Helsinki
Population 5,238,460

Iceland
Capital City Reykjavik
Population 301,931

Latvia
Capital City Riga
Population 2,259,810

Lithuania
Capital City Vilnius
Population 3,575,439

Norway
Capital City Oslo
Population 4,627,926

Sweden
Capital City Stockholm
Population 9,031,088

Western Europe p.34

Andorra
Capital City Andorra la Vella
Population 71,822

Belgium
Capital City Brussels
Population 10,392,226

France
Capital City Paris
Population 63,713,926

Ireland
Capital City Dublin
Population 4,109,086

Luxembourg
Capital City Luxembourg
Population 480,222

Monaco
Capital City Monaco-Ville
Population 32,671

Netherlands
Capital Cities Amsterdam and The Hague
Population 16,570,613

Portugal
Capital City Lisbon
Population 10,642,836

Spain
Capital City Madrid
Population 40,448,191

United Kingdom
Capital City London
Population 60,776,238

Central Europe p36

Austria
Capital City Vienna
Population 8,199,783

Czech Republic
Capital City Prague
Population 10,228,744

Germany
Capital City Berlin
Population 82,400,996

Italy
Capital City Rome
Population 58,147,733

Liechtenstein
Capital City Vaduz
Population 34,247

Malta
Capital City Valletta
Population 401,880

Poland
Capital City Warsaw
Population 38,518,241

San Marino
Capital City San Marino
Population 29,615

Slovakia
Capital City Bratislava
Population 5,447,502

Slovenia
Capital City Ljubljana
Population 2,009,245

Switzerland
Capital City Bern
Population 7,554,661

Vatican City
Capital City Vatican City
Population 821

Southeast Europe p.38

Albania
Capital City Tirana
Population 3,600,523

Belarus
Capital City Minsk
Population 9,724,723

Bosnia and Herzegovina
Capital City Sarajevo
Population 4,552,198

Bulgaria
Capital City Sofia
Population 7,322,858

Croatia
Capital City Zagreb
Population 4,493,312

Greece
Capital City Athens
Population 10,706,290

Hungary
Capital City Budapest
Population 9,956,108

Macedonia
Capital City Skopje
Population 2,055,915

Moldova
Capital City Chisinau
Population 4,320,490

Montenegro
Capital City Podgorica
Population 684,736

Romania
Capital City Bucharest
Population 22,276,056

Serbia
Capital City Belgrade
Population 10,150,265

Ukraine
Capital City Kiev
Population 46,299,862

Russian Federation p.40

Russian Federation
Capital City Moscow
Population 141,377,752

ASIA
Southwest Asia p.42

Armenia
Capital City Yerevan
Population 2,971,650

Azerbaijan
Capital City Baku
Population 8,120,247

Bahrain
Capital City Manama
Population 708,573

Cyprus
Capital City Nicosia
Population 788,457

Georgia
Capital City T'bilisi
Population 4,646,003

Iran
Capital City Tehran
Population 65,397,521

Iraq
Capital City Baghdad
Population 27,499,638

Israel
Capital City Jerusalem
Population 6,426,679

Jordan
Capital City Amman
Population 6,053,193

Kuwait
Capital City Kuwait
Population 2,505,559

Lebanon
Capital City Beirut
Population 3,925,502

Oman
Capital City Muscat
Population 3,204,897

Qatar
Capital City Doha
Population 907,229

Saudi Arabia
Capital City Riyadh
Population 27,601,038

Syria
Capital City Damascus
Population 19,314,747

Turkey
Capital City Ankara
Population 71,158,647

United Arab Emirates
Capital City Abu Dhabi
Population 4,444,011

Yemen
Capital City Sana
Population 22,230,531

Central Asia p.44

Afghanistan
Capital City Kabul
Population 31,889,923

Kazakhstan
Capital City Astana
Population 15,284,929

Kyrgyzstan
Capital City Bishkek
Population 5,284,149

Tajikistan
Capital City Dushanbe
Population 7,076,598

Turkmenistan
Capital City Asgabat
Population 5,097,028

Uzbekistan
Capital City Tashkent
Population 27,780,059

South Asia p.46

Bangladesh
Capital City Dhaka
Population 150,448,339

Bhutan
Capital City Thimphu
Population 2,327,849

India
Capital City New Delhi
Population 1,129,866,154

Maldives
Capital City Male
Population 369,031

Nepal
Capital City Kathmandu
Population 28,901,790

Pakistan
Capital City Islamabad
Population 164,741,924

Sri Lanka
Capital City Colombo
Population 20,926,315

East Asia p.48

China
Capital City Beijing
Population 1,321,851,888

Japan
Capital City Tokyo
Population 127,433,494

Mongolia
Capital City Ulan Bator
Population 2,951,786

North Korea
Capital City Pyongyang
Population 23,301,725

South Korea
Capital City Seoul
Population 49,044,790

Taiwan
Capital City Taipei
Population 22,858,872

Southeast Asia p.50

Brunei
Capital City Bandar Seri Begawan
Population 374,577

Burma
Capital City Naypyidaw
Population 47,373,958

Cambodia
Capital City Phnom Penh
Population 13,995,904

East Timor
Capital City Dili
Population 1,084,971

Indonesia
Capital City Jakarta
Population 234,693,997

Laos
Capital City Vientiane
Population 6,521,998

Malaysia
Capital City Kuala Lumpur
Population 24,821,286

Philippines
Capital City Manila
Population 91,077,287

Singapore
Capital City Singapore
Population 4,553,009

Thailand
Capital City Bangkok
Population 65,068,149

Vietnam
Capital City Ha Noi
Population 85,262,356

AUSTRALASIA AND OCEANIA
Australia p.52

Australia
Capital City Canberra
Population 20,434,176

Pacific Islands p.54

Fiji
Capital City Suva
Population 918,675

Kiribati
Capital City Bairiki
Population 107,817

Marshall Islands
Capital City Majuro
Population 61,815

Micronesia
Capital City Palikir
Population 107,862

Nauru
Capital City no official capital
Population 13,528

Palau
Capital City Oreor
Population 20,842

Papua New Guinea
Capital City Port Moresby
Population 5,795,887

Samoa
Capital City Apia
Population 214,265

Solomon Islands
Capital City Honiara
Population 566,842

Tonga
Capital City Nuku'alofa
Population 116,921

Tuvalu
Capital City Fongafale
Population 11,992

Vanuatu
Capital City Port-Vila
Population 211,971

New Zealand p.56

New Zealand
Capital City Wellington
Population 4,115,771

ANTARCTICA p.59
The continent of Antarctica is unusual. It has no countries and no-one lives there all year round because it is so cold.

Canada
NORTH AMERICA

This is the second biggest country in the world (the largest is the Russian Federation), and it is part of North America. In southern Canada, wheat and other crops grow on the Great Plains. Further north are thick coniferous forests and many rivers and lakes. Near the Arctic Circle, in the north, is a huge area of tundra, which turns marshy in summer, and inside the Arctic Circle the ground is always frozen. Most of the 33 million people in Canada live in the south, within 160 kilometres of the border with the USA. The weather is milder there and travelling is easier. The population is made up mostly of the descendants of Europeans who settled there from the 16th century, plus the original First Nations people. Canada is rich in minerals and fossil fuels, and mining is an important industry. Other industries are fishing, agriculture and machinery, car, timber and paper manufacturing.

Country File
Canada

The maple leaf is the national symbol of Canada

ARCTIC OCEAN

Beaufort Sea

Banks Island

Victoria Island

UNITED STATES OF AMERICA (Alaska)

Arctic Circle

Yukon

MACKENZIE MOUNTAINS

Great Bear Lake

YUKON TERRITORY

Mount Logan 5959m ▲

Whitehorse

NORTHWEST TERRITORIES

Yellowknife

Great Slave Lake

Mackenzie

Lake Athabasca

Peace

ROCKY MOUNTAINS

CANADA

ALBERTA

Reindeer Lake

PACIFIC OCEAN

Queen Charlotte Islands

BRITISH COLUMBIA

Prince George

GREAT PLAINS

Edmonton

SASKATCHEWAN

Athabasca

Saskatchewan

Fraser

Red Deer

Calgary

Saskatoon

Vancouver Island

Kamloops

Vancouver

Kelowna

Nanaimo

Victoria

Lethbridge

Medicine Hat

Regina

UNITED STATES OF

| 0 | 250 | 500 kilometres |
| 0 | 250 | 500 mi |

Beaver
The American beaver is the largest rodent in North America and it can measure 1.35 metres from nose to tail. Beavers build dams across rivers to form lakes, where they are safe from predators such as wolves and bears. Their dams are made from logs, sticks and mud. Beavers then build homes in the lake called lodges.

Lakes and forests
There are thousands of freshwater lakes and rivers in Canada, and almost half of the country is covered in forest. Wood products, especially wood pulp and paper, make up a large part of Canada's export trade.

Ellesmere Island

G R E E N L A N D

abeth Islands

Baffin Bay

Davis Strait

Did you know?

◈ One of the fastest-growing women's sports in the world is ice hockey. In 2006, the Canadian women's team won the Olympic gold medal, beating Sweden in the final. Ice hockey is the most widely watched sport in Canada.

Baffin Island

N U N A V U T

Iqaluit ★

Southampton Island

Hudson Strait

Did you know?

◈ Canada has two official languages – French and English.

◈ Canada produces more hydroelectricity than any other nation in the world, except China.

UNGAVA PENINSULA

Ungava Bay

Labrador Sea

Hudson Bay

A D A

N E W F O U N D L A N D A N D L A B R A D O R

Churchill

Smallwood Reservoir

La Grande Reservoir

M A N I T O B A

James Bay

Q U É B E C

LAURENTIAN MOUNTAINS

St John's ★

Newfoundland

N

O N T A R I O

S H I E L D

Lake Winnipeg

Anticosti Island

Gulf of St Lawrence

ST PIERRE & MIQUELON (to France)

PRINCE EDWARD ISLAND

Lake Nipigon

Chicoutimi ●

NEW BRUNSWICK

Charlottetown ★

Winnipeg ★

Fredericton ● ● Moncton

Thunder Bay ●

Québec ★

Saint John ★

Trois-Rivières ●

★ Halifax

M E R I C A

Lake Superior

Sudbury ●

Montreal ●

Sherbrooke ●

NOVA SCOTIA

Sault Ste Marie ●

St Lawrence

Canada 🍁

Lake Huron

OTTAWA ★

Bay of Fundy

A T L A N T I C   O C E A N

Did you know?

◈ Lake Superior is the largest freshwater lake in the world by area. It is 83,270 sq km – almost as big as Austria.

◈ Canada is famous for maple syrup, which is made from the sap of the maple tree.

Lake Michigan

Toronto ★   Oshawa ●
Lake Ontario

Kitchener ●   ● St Catharines

London ●   Hamilton ●
Niagara Falls

Windsor ●

Lake Erie

To find out more about Canada go to:
www.pandg-atlas.com

Salmon fishing

The cold waters around the coast of Canada are rich in fish, including cod and salmon. Salmon is very important to the Canadian fishing industry, and tinned salmon is exported around the world.

Moose

The moose is about 2 metres tall at the shoulder and is the biggest deer in the world. It roams through most of Canada, eating young trees and shrubs. Its name came from a Native American word, *mus* or *moos*, which means 'twig eater'.

CN Tower

At 553.33 metres high, Canada's National Tower in Toronto is the world's tallest free-standing tower. It is one of the greatest feats of engineering. From the top you can see as far as 160 kilometres away.

United States of America
NORTH AMERICA

The United States of America (USA) covers an area almost the size of Europe. It includes the states of Alaska at the northwest tip of Canada and Hawaii in the Pacific Ocean. The land and climate of the USA change dramatically across this huge area. There are deserts, mountains, prairie lands and swamps. In Alaska there is permanent snow and temperatures drop to below -30°C in winter. In the southeast the temperature rarely drops below 10°C. The population of over 301 million contains people descended from immigrants from all over the world, especially Europe. There are also 2.4 million Native American people. The USA is one of the world's wealthiest nations. There are huge oil and gas fields in Texas and Oklahoma, minerals are mined in Montana and Wyoming, and California is a centre for the computer industry. Some of the world's best wine is also made in California.

Country File

United States of America

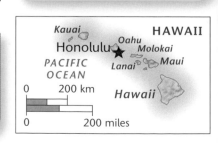

Detroit has been home to the USA's motor industry since Henry Ford built his first vehicle there in 1896.

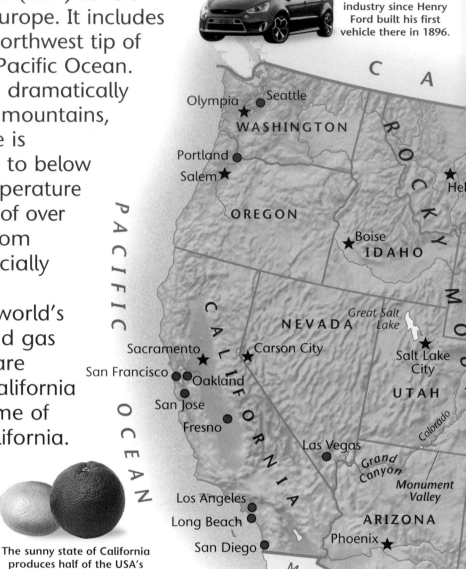

The sunny state of California produces half of the USA's fruit and vegetables.

Monument Valley
The great 'buttes' of Monument Valley, on the border of Utah and Arizona, were formed by rivers, rain and wind, which have eroded the soft rock around them over millions of years. The land between the buttes was once as high as they are. Their red colour comes from iron oxide in the soil, which is also known as rust.

0   200   400 kilometres
0   200   400 m

Did you know?

◇ The Grand Canyon in Arizona is one of the natural wonders of the world. It is up to 1,800m deep and was cut out by the Colorado river over many millions of years.

Did you know?

◇ The largest oil field in the USA is in Prudhoe Bay, Alaska. But the ground there is frozen for most of the year, which makes it difficult to drill for oil.

◇ The 16 highest mountains in the United States of America are all in Alaska.

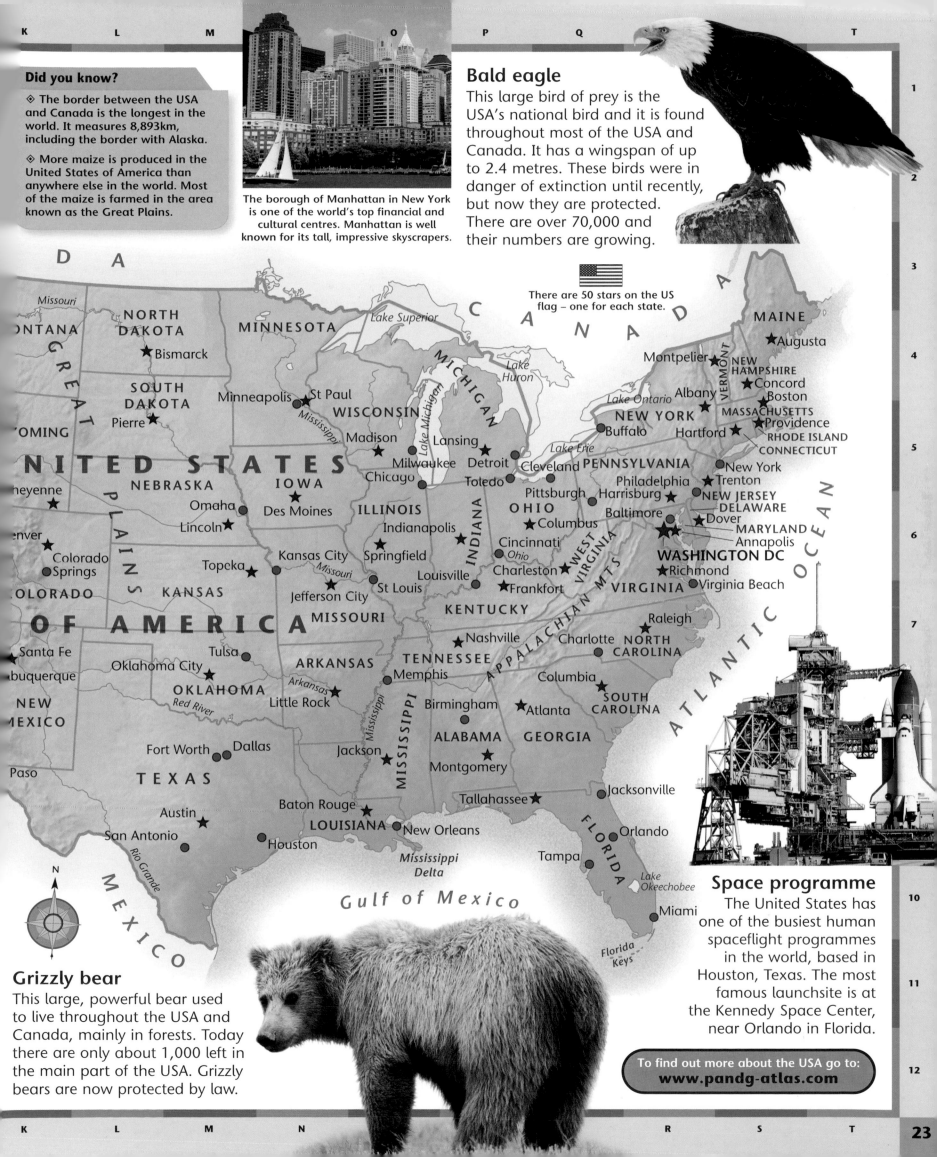

Did you know?

◇ The border between the USA and Canada is the longest in the world. It measures 8,893km, including the border with Alaska.

◇ More maize is produced in the United States of America than anywhere else in the world. Most of the maize is farmed in the area known as the Great Plains.

The borough of Manhattan in New York is one of the world's top financial and cultural centres. Manhattan is well known for its tall, impressive skyscrapers.

Bald eagle

This large bird of prey is the USA's national bird and it is found throughout most of the USA and Canada. It has a wingspan of up to 2.4 metres. These birds were in danger of extinction until recently, but now they are protected. There are over 70,000 and their numbers are growing.

There are 50 stars on the US flag – one for each state.

Map labels

CANADA

Missouri

MONTANA
NORTH DAKOTA
★ Bismarck

MINNESOTA

Lake Superior

MICHIGAN

Lake Huron

MAINE
★ Augusta

GREAT

SOUTH DAKOTA
★ Pierre

Minneapolis ★ St Paul

WISCONSIN

Lake Michigan

Montpelier
VERMONT
NEW HAMPSHIRE
★ Concord
★ Boston

WYOMING

Madison ★

Lansing ★

Lake Ontario
Albany ★

MASSACHUSETTS
★ Providence
RHODE ISLAND
CONNECTICUT

UNITED STATES

NEBRASKA

IOWA
★

Milwaukee
Chicago

Detroit
Toledo

Lake Erie
Cleveland

PENNSYLVANIA
Buffalo

Hartford ★

New York

Cheyenne

Omaha
Lincoln ★

Des Moines ★

ILLINOIS
Indianapolis ★

INDIANA

OHIO
★ Columbus

Pittsburgh
Harrisburg ★

Philadelphia

Trenton
NEW JERSEY
DELAWARE

Denver

Colorado Springs

PLAINS

Topeka ★

Kansas City

Springfield ★

Missouri

Cincinnati
Ohio

WEST VIRGINIA

Baltimore
Dover

MARYLAND
Annapolis

COLORADO

KANSAS

St Louis

Louisville

Charleston

★ WASHINGTON DC

OF AMERICA

Jefferson City ★

MISSOURI

KENTUCKY
★ Frankfort

VIRGINIA
★ Richmond

Virginia Beach

Santa Fe

Tulsa

Nashville ★

APPALACHIAN MTS

Raleigh ★

ATLANTIC OCEAN

Albuquerque

Oklahoma City

ARKANSAS

TENNESSEE

Charlotte
NORTH CAROLINA

NEW MEXICO

OKLAHOMA
Red River

Arkansas

Memphis

Columbia ★

SOUTH CAROLINA

El Paso

Little Rock ★

Mississippi

Birmingham
★ Atlanta

Fort Worth
Dallas

Jackson ★

ALABAMA

GEORGIA

TEXAS

MISSISSIPPI

Montgomery ★

Tallahassee ★

Jacksonville

Austin ★

Baton Rouge ★

LOUISIANA
New Orleans

Orlando

FLORIDA

San Antonio

Rio Grande

Houston

Tampa

Lake Okeechobee

N

MEXICO

Mississippi Delta

Gulf of Mexico

Miami

Florida Keys

Grizzly bear

This large, powerful bear used to live throughout the USA and Canada, mainly in forests. Today there are only about 1,000 left in the main part of the USA. Grizzly bears are now protected by law.

Space programme

The United States has one of the busiest human spaceflight programmes in the world, based in Houston, Texas. The most famous launchsite is at the Kennedy Space Center, near Orlando in Florida.

To find out more about the USA go to:
www.pandg-atlas.com

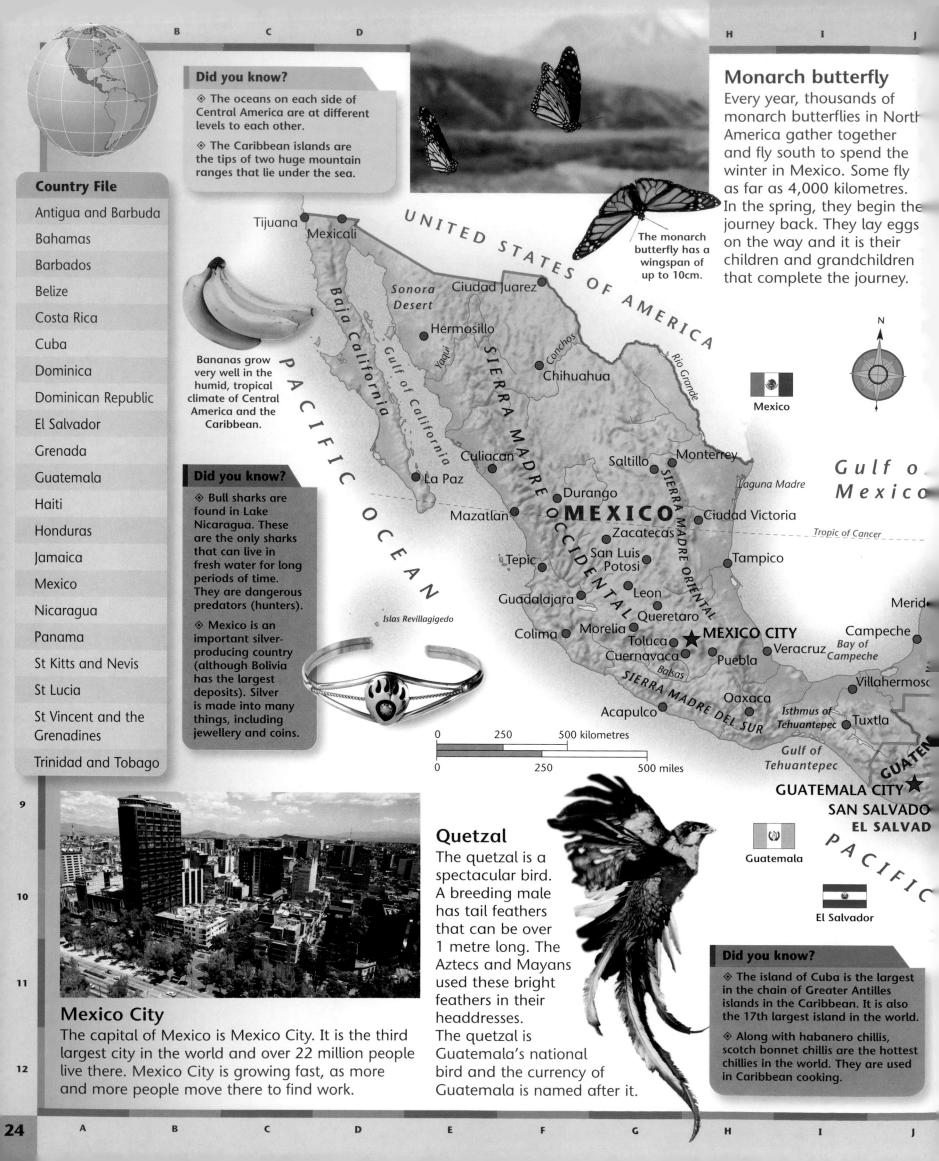

Country File

Antigua and Barbuda

Bahamas

Barbados

Belize

Costa Rica

Cuba

Dominica

Dominican Republic

El Salvador

Grenada

Guatemala

Haiti

Honduras

Jamaica

Mexico

Nicaragua

Panama

St Kitts and Nevis

St Lucia

St Vincent and the Grenadines

Trinidad and Tobago

Did you know?

◈ The oceans on each side of Central America are at different levels to each other.

◈ The Caribbean islands are the tips of two huge mountain ranges that lie under the sea.

Monarch butterfly

Every year, thousands of monarch butterflies in North America gather together and fly south to spend the winter in Mexico. Some fly as far as 4,000 kilometres. In the spring, they begin the journey back. They lay eggs on the way and it is their children and grandchildren that complete the journey.

The monarch butterfly has a wingspan of up to 10cm.

Bananas grow very well in the humid, tropical climate of Central America and the Caribbean.

Did you know?

◈ Bull sharks are found in Lake Nicaragua. These are the only sharks that can live in fresh water for long periods of time. They are dangerous predators (hunters).

◈ Mexico is an important silver-producing country (although Bolivia has the largest deposits). Silver is made into many things, including jewellery and coins.

Mexico

UNITED STATES OF AMERICA

Tijuana
Mexicali

PACIFIC OCEAN

Baja California

Sonora Desert

Ciudad Juarez

Gulf of California

Yaqui

Conchos

Chihuahua

Hermosillo

SIERRA MADRE OCCIDENTAL

Rio Grande

La Paz

Culiacan

Saltillo   Monterrey

Laguna Madre

Durango

Mazatlan   **MEXICO**   Ciudad Victoria

SIERRA MADRE ORIENTAL

Zacatecas

Tropic of Cancer

Tepic

San Luis Potosi

Tampico

Guadalajara   Leon

Islas Revillagigedo

Colima   Morelia   Queretaro

Merid

Toluca   **MEXICO CITY**   Campeche

Cuernavaca   Puebla   Veracruz   Bay of Campeche

Balsas

SIERRA MADRE DEL SUR   Villahermoso

Acapulco   Oaxaca

Isthmus of Tehuantepec   Tuxtla

Gulf of Tehuantepec

GUATE

Gulf of Mexico

N

Mexico

0   250   500 kilometres

0   250   500 miles

GUATEMALA CITY

SAN SALVADO

EL SALVAD

Guatemala

PACIFIC

El Salvador

Quetzal

The quetzal is a spectacular bird. A breeding male has tail feathers that can be over 1 metre long. The Aztecs and Mayans used these bright feathers in their headdresses. The quetzal is Guatemala's national bird and the currency of Guatemala is named after it.

Mexico City

The capital of Mexico is Mexico City. It is the third largest city in the world and over 22 million people live there. Mexico City is growing fast, as more and more people move there to find work.

Did you know?

◈ The island of Cuba is the largest in the chain of Greater Antilles islands in the Caribbean. It is also the 17th largest island in the world.

◈ Along with habanero chillis, scotch bonnet chillis are the hottest chillies in the world. They are used in Caribbean cooking.

Central America and the Caribbean

NORTH AMERICA

The continents of North and South America are linked by a narrow piece of land called Central America. To the east are the Greater and Lesser Antilles islands, which are also known as the Caribbean islands. All along Central America there are mountains and volcanoes. In the north there are hot, dry deserts and in the south there are tropical rainforests. The Caribbean also has rainforests and a tropical climate. Most of the people who live in this region are descended from Africans, Asians and Europeans. In Central America, fishing, coffee and fruit growing are important industries, and most of Mexico's income comes from oil and gas. Tourism and sugar farming are important in the Caribbean.

Caribbean islands

St Lucia, Antigua and the other islands of the Caribbean are popular holiday destinations. Many tourists are attracted by the warm, clear sea, sandy beaches and tropical climate.

Bahamas
Cuba
NASSAU
Andros Island
BAHAMAS
ATLANTIC OCEAN
HAVANA   Matanzas
Pinar del Rio
CUBA
Camaguey
Cancun
Isla Cozumel
Greater
GUANTANAMO BAY (to US)
Santiago de Cuba
Hispaniola
TURKS & CAICOS ISLANDS (to UK)
CAYMAN ISLANDS (to UK)
HAITI
DOMINICAN REPUBLIC
PORT-AU-PRINCE
SANTO DOMINGO
PUERTO RICO (to US)
SAN JUAN
VIRGIN ISLANDS (to US)
BRITISH VIRGIN ISLANDS (to UK)
ANGUILLA (to UK)
ANTIGUA & BARBUDA
ST KITTS & NEVIS
MONTSERRAT (to UK)
GUADELOUPE (to France)
DOMINICA
MARTINIQUE (to France)
ST LUCIA
BARBADOS
ST VINCENT & THE GRENADINES
GRENADA
Tobago
TRINIDAD & TOBAGO
Leeward Islands
Windward Islands
Lesser Antilles
Antilles
Antigua and Barbuda
Dominica
Barbados
Belize
Belize City
BELMOPAN BELIZE
Honduras
Jamaica
JAMAICA
KINGSTON
Haiti
Dominican Republic
St Kitts and Nevis
St Lucia
HONDURAS
TEGUCIGALPA
Caribbean Sea
ARUBA (to Netherlands)
NETHERLANDS ANTILLES (to Netherlands)
NICARAGUA
MANAGUA
Lake Nicaragua
Leon
Nicaragua
Panama
COLOMBIA
VENEZUELA
Trinidad and Tobago
Grenada
St Vincent and the Grenadines
SAN JOSE
Limon
Colon
Panama Canal
Gulf of Darien
PANAMA CITY
COSTA RICA
PANAMA
OCEAN
Costa Rica

Panama Canal

The Pacific and Atlantic Oceans are linked by the Panama Canal. This waterway is about 80 kilometres long. By using the canal, a boat travelling from one coast of North America to the other can avoid going around Cape Horn in South America and cut its journey by about 15,000 kilometres.

To find out more about Central America and the Carribean go to:
www.pandg-atlas.com

South America
SOUTH AMERICA

The continent of South America is home to the Amazon rainforest and mountains of the Andes. The Amazon River is about 6,500 kilometres long and is the greatest river in South America. The climate ranges from tropical in the north to bitterly cold in the south – the tip of South America is only 1,000 kilometres away from Antarctica. In between, the climate is less extreme. There are wide, open grasslands called the Pampas, where cattle and cereals are farmed. Northern South America is rich in oil and gas, especially in Venezuela. Further south, copper and iron ore are found. Coffee is the most important crop in South America, and Brazil is the world's leading coffee grower. Cocoa, sugarcane and bananas are also important crops. Most of the population is descended from Europeans, Amerindians or Africans.

Country File

- Argentina
- Bolivia
- Brazil
- Chile
- Colombia
- Ecuador
- Guyana
- Paraguay
- Peru
- Suriname
- Uruguay
- Venezuela

Angel Falls
The highest waterfall in the world is the Angel Falls in Venezuela. Angel Falls is almost 1 kilometre high – 19 times higher than the Niagara Falls on the USA and Canada border.

Did you know?

◈ Bolivia has two capital cities – La Paz and Sucre. La Paz is 3,600m above sea level, which makes it the highest capital city in the world.

◈ Ecuador exports more bananas than any other country in the world.

◈ The Amazon rainforest is over half the size of the United States of America.

◈ The grass in the Pampas region grows up to 3m tall. It has long, thin, sharp leaves and big, fluffy flowerheads.

Carnival time
Every year, just before Lent, 'Carnival' begins in Rio de Janeiro, Brazil. For five days people dress up, dance and parade through the streets to the sound of samba music. There is a competition for the most outrageous costume and the best decorated float.

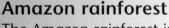

Many of the best known vegetables in the world, such as tomatoes, potatoes, beans and corn, originally came from South America.

Amazon rainforest
The Amazon rainforest is the largest tropical rainforest in the world. Many scientists believe that more than one-third of all the world's species of plants and animals live there. About 1.5 square kilometres of Brazilian rainforest are destroyed every hour, as the forest is cut down for timber and cleared for farming. If this continues, the rainforest will eventually be gone. Hundreds of thousands of species of animals and plants will be lost for ever.

Jaguar
For its size, the jaguar is one of the strongest mammals in the world. This cat can kill prey over three times its own body weight. It is good at climbing, crawling and swimming, which are useful skills in its rainforest habitat.

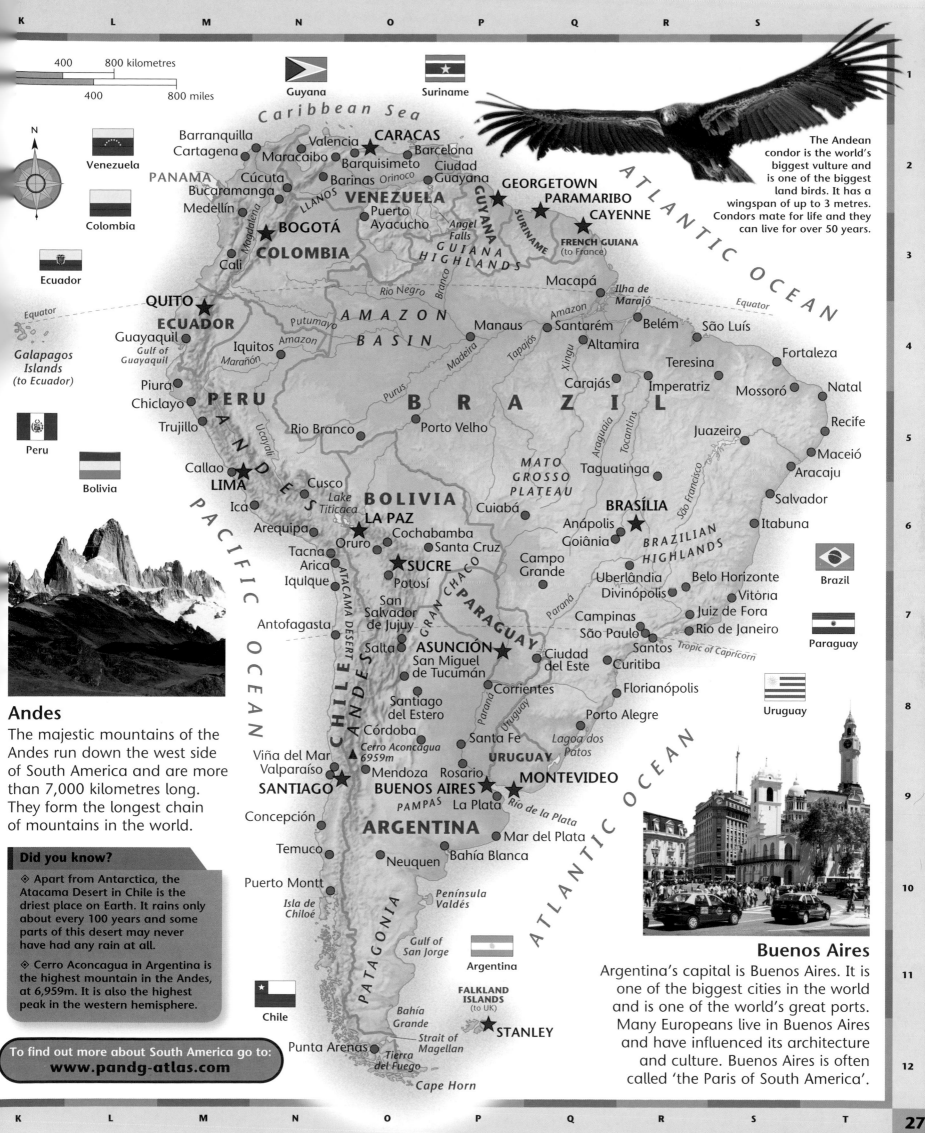

The Andean condor is the world's biggest vulture and is one of the biggest land birds. It has a wingspan of up to 3 metres. Condors mate for life and they can live for over 50 years.

Andes

The majestic mountains of the Andes run down the west side of South America and are more than 7,000 kilometres long. They form the longest chain of mountains in the world.

Did you know?

◇ Apart from Antarctica, the Atacama Desert in Chile is the driest place on Earth. It rains only about every 100 years and some parts of this desert may never have had any rain at all.

◇ Cerro Aconcagua in Argentina is the highest mountain in the Andes, at 6,959m. It is also the highest peak in the western hemisphere.

To find out more about South America go to:
www.pandg-atlas.com

Buenos Aires

Argentina's capital is Buenos Aires. It is one of the biggest cities in the world and is one of the world's great ports. Many Europeans live in Buenos Aires and have influenced its architecture and culture. Buenos Aires is often called 'the Paris of South America'.

Northern Africa

AFRICA

The continent of Africa is the second largest in the world (Asia is the biggest). Northern Africa is mostly covered by the Sahara, which is the world's largest hot desert. Few people live there because conditions are so harsh. Most people in Northern Africa live near the coast or along the River Nile. Crops such as dates, cork, grapes and olives are produced in the north of the region, and cocoa, groundnuts (peanuts) and palm oil in the south. Textiles are made in every area, especially in the north, where rugs are produced. There are big deposits of oil and natural gas in Libya, and in countries such as Egypt, Tunisia and Morocco, tourism is important.

Country File

Algeria

Benin

Burkina Faso

Cameroon

Cape Verde

Central African Republic

Chad

Djibouti

Egypt

Eritrea

Ethiopia

Gambia

Ghana

Guinea

Guinea-Bissau

Ivory Coast

Liberia

Libya

Mali

Mauritania

Morocco

Niger

Nigeria

Senegal

Sierra Leone

Somalia

Sudan

Togo

Tunisia

Western Sahara

Did you know?

◇ Uranium, diamonds and gold are mined in northern Africa. There are also reserves of oil and natural gas in this area.

Did you know?

◇ Half of the world's cocoa beans are now grown in Northern Africa, even though the cocoa bean originally came from South America.

Tunisia

Algeria

Morocco

Western Sahara

Mauritania

Mali

Cape Verde

Senegal

Gambia

Guinea-Bissau

Guinea

Sierra Leone

Liberia

Ivory Coast

Burkina Faso

Ghana

Togo

Benin

Nigeria

Mediter

ALGIERS   TUNIS

Tanger   Oran   Constantine

RABAT   Casablanca   Sfa

MOROCCO   ATLAS MOUNTAINS   **TUNISI**

Marrakech

ATLANTIC OCEAN

LAAYOUNE

WESTERN SAHARA   *Tropic of Cancer*   **ALGERIA**

AHAGGAR

S A H A R A

MAURITANIA

NOUAKCHOTT   **MALI**   **NIGER**

Senegal   Agadez

CAPE VERDE   *Niger*   **S A H E L**

PRAIA   **SENEGAL**

DAKAR   BAMAKO   NIAMEY

GAMBIA   OUAGADOUGOU

BANJUL   **BURKINA FASO**

BISSAU   **NIGERIA**

GUINEA-BISSAU   **GUINEA**

CONAKRY   **IVORY COAST**   ABUJA

FREETOWN   YAMOUSSOUKRO   PORTO-NOVO

SIERRA LEONE   Lagos

MONROVIA   **LIBERIA**   Abidjan   ACCRA   LOME   Douala

Gulf of Guinea   YAOUND

EQUATORIAL GUINEA

Fennec fox

This mammal is suited to life in the hot desert. Its sandy colour helps it to hide from prey, and it keeps cool by losing body heat through its huge ears. This fox usually hunts at night when it is cooler.

0   400   800 kilometres

0   400   800 miles

12

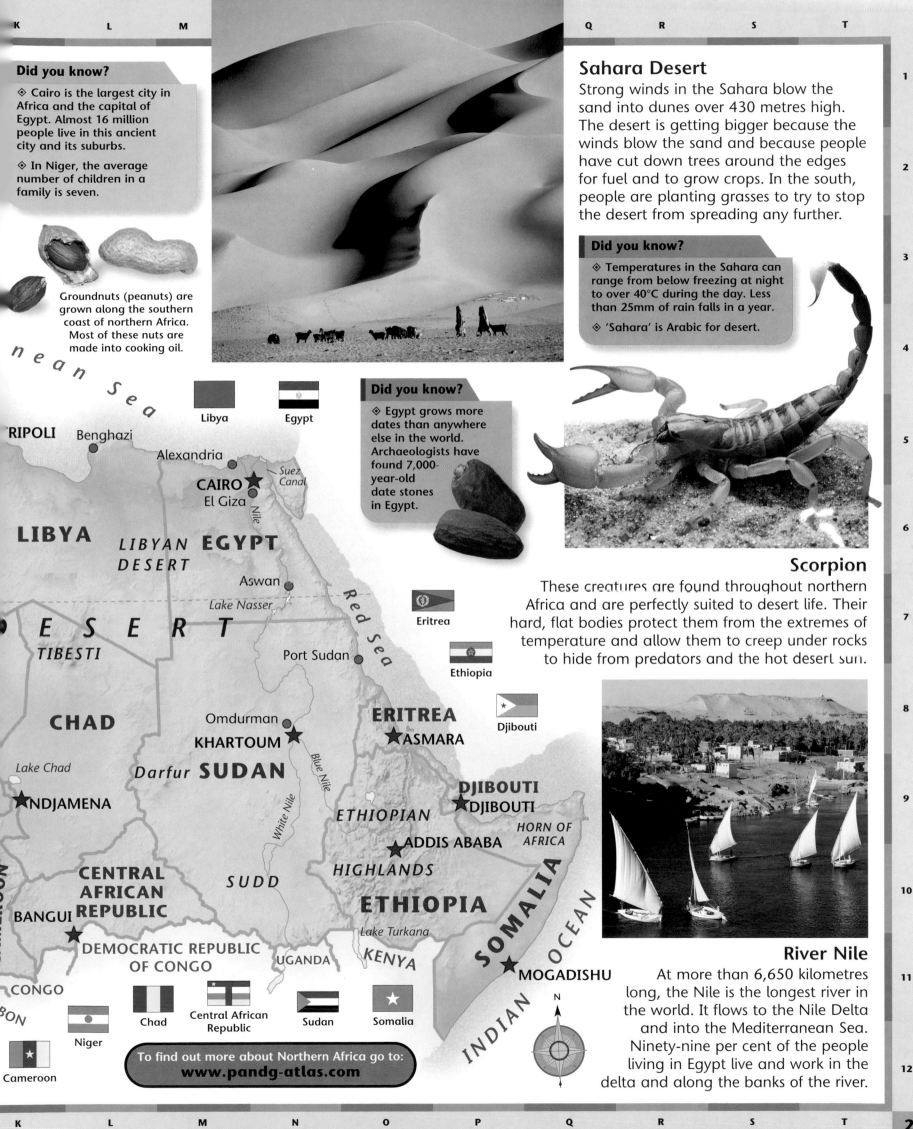

Did you know?

◇ Cairo is the largest city in Africa and the capital of Egypt. Almost 16 million people live in this ancient city and its suburbs.

◇ In Niger, the average number of children in a family is seven.

Groundnuts (peanuts) are grown along the southern coast of northern Africa. Most of these nuts are made into cooking oil.

Sahara Desert

Strong winds in the Sahara blow the sand into dunes over 430 metres high. The desert is getting bigger because the winds blow the sand and because people have cut down trees around the edges for fuel and to grow crops. In the south, people are planting grasses to try to stop the desert from spreading any further.

Did you know?

◇ Temperatures in the Sahara can range from below freezing at night to over 40°C during the day. Less than 25mm of rain falls in a year.

◇ 'Sahara' is Arabic for desert.

Did you know?

◇ Egypt grows more dates than anywhere else in the world. Archaeologists have found 7,000-year-old date stones in Egypt.

Scorpion

These creatures are found throughout northern Africa and are perfectly suited to desert life. Their hard, flat bodies protect them from the extremes of temperature and allow them to creep under rocks to hide from predators and the hot desert sun.

River Nile

At more than 6,650 kilometres long, the Nile is the longest river in the world. It flows to the Nile Delta and into the Mediterranean Sea. Ninety-nine per cent of the people living in Egypt live and work in the delta and along the banks of the river.

Map labels:

nean Sea
TRIPOLI
Benghazi
Alexandria
Suez Canal
CAIRO
El Giza
Nile
Libya
Egypt
LIBYA
LIBYAN DESERT
EGYPT
Aswan
Lake Nasser
Red Sea
DESERT
TIBESTI
Port Sudan
Eritrea
Ethiopia
CHAD
Omdurman
KHARTOUM
ERITREA
ASMARA
Djibouti
Lake Chad
Darfur SUDAN
Blue Nile
NDJAMENA
White Nile
DJIBOUTI
DJIBOUTI
HORN OF AFRICA
ETHIOPIAN
ADDIS ABABA
CENTRAL AFRICAN REPUBLIC
SUDD
HIGHLANDS
ETHIOPIA
SOMALIA
BANGUI
DEMOCRATIC REPUBLIC OF CONGO
Lake Turkana
UGANDA
KENYA
INDIAN OCEAN
CONGO
MOGADISHU
GABON
Niger
Chad
Central African Republic
Sudan
Somalia
Cameroon
CAMEROON

To find out more about Northern Africa go to:
www.pandg-atlas.com

N

Southern Africa
AFRICA

Southern Africa has many different climates. The Congo Basin is hot and humid and is the site of the world's second biggest tropical rainforest (the Amazon forest in South America is the largest). Further east and south are dry woodlands merging into savannah, which is a mixture of grassland and open woodland. It is there that the most well known African animals are found. Further south is the Namib Desert, one of the hottest and driest places on Earth, with temperatures over 50°C during the day. Hundreds of different tribes live in southern Africa, and there are hundreds of languages. The Kalahari Desert in Botswana is home to one of the few remaining groups of hunter gatherers, the Bushmen, or San. In the 19th century, large gold and diamond deposits were found in South Africa, helping it to become the most powerful country in Southern Africa.

Country File

- Angola
- Botswana
- Burundi
- Comoros
- Congo
- Democratic Republic of Congo
- Equatorial Guinea
- Gabon
- Kenya
- Lesotho
- Madagascar
- Malawi
- Mauritius
- Mozambique
- Namibia
- Rwanda
- Sao Tome and Principe
- Seychelles
- South Africa
- Swaziland
- Tanzania
- Uganda
- Zambia
- Zimbabwe

Many different crops are grown in Southern Africa, including citrus fruits and grapes, mainly for export

Equatorial Guinea

Congo

Sao Tome and Principe

Gabon

Angola

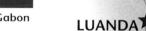

Namibia

Botswana

South Africa

Victoria Falls

This famous waterfall is on the Zambezi River, on the border between Zambia and Zimbabwe. It is 108 metres high and 1,700 metres wide. David Livingstone was the first European to see it, in 1855. He named it for Queen Victoria of England. Local people call it 'the smoke that thunders' because of the loud noise and spray that it makes.

African wildlife

Elephants, rhinoceroses, lions, leopards and buffalo are known as 'the big five' and they attract thousands of tourists to Africa. These animals used to be shot for sport and were the five most dangerous animals, but now they are shot with cameras! Many are endangered species and they are protected by law.

Did you know?

◇ There are two species of elephant in Africa. The African bush elephant lives on the savannah and the smaller forest elephant lives in tropical rainforests.

◇ Half of all the world's diamonds are mined in Southern Africa.

Map labels

MALABO
EQUATORIAL GUINEA
CAMEROON
CENTRAL AFR
SAO TOME
SAO TOME & PRINCIPE
LIBREVILLE
GABON
Mbandaka
CONGO
DE
RE
BRAZZAVILLE
KINSHASA
ANGOLA
Kanar
LUANDA
ANGOLA
Huambo
BIÉ PLATEAU
Namibe
Lubango
ATLANTIC OCEAN
NAMIBIA
WINDHOEK
NAMIB DESERT
KALAHA
DESER
Orange River
SOUT
CAPE TOWN
Cape of Good Hope

Did you know?

◇ Although many African countries produce a large variety of crops, most people live off a few crops, such as yams and cassava.

◇ Most animals living in rainforests are small, and each kind of animal usually eats one type of food.

Congo, Democratic Republic of

Uganda

Kenya

Gorillas are the largest primates in the world (humans are primates too). These apes live in forests, in groups led by a large male.

Did you know?

◇ The book (and film) *Gorillas in the Mist* is about rare mountain gorillas in Rwanda. It is by Dian Fossey, a zoologist who died trying to protect gorillas in the wild.

◇ The Okavango River never reaches the sea. Instead, its waters flood a huge area in northern Botswana called the Okavango Delta. This area is full of wildlife.

Rwanda

Burundi

Tanzania

Seychelles

Comoros

Malawi

Zambia

Mauritius

Madagascar

Zimbabwe

Mozambique

Swaziland

Lesotho

Kilimanjaro

The top of Kilimanjaro in Tanzania is covered in snow all year round, even though the mountain is close to the Equator. This is because the temperature drops as the land gets higher. Kilimanjaro is 5,895 metres high and it is the highest point in Africa.

Baobab tree

The island of Madagascar, off the eastern coast of Africa, split off from the mainland millions of years ago. Many unusual species of plants and animals developed there, and it is the only place on Earth where certain species of plants and animals can be found. Several types of baobab tree grow only in Madagascar. Some of these extraordinary trees are over 3,000 years old.

South Africa's climate is varied and is suitable for growing many types of cut flower, such as gerberas (shown here), roses and carnations. These are all exported to Europe, as well as being sold locally.

Did you know?

◇ The earliest known human fossils were found in the Olduvai Gorge in the Great Rift Valley in Tanzania. They are about 2.3 million years old. Many people think that this is where humans first evolved. The gorge is often called 'the cradle of mankind'.

To find out more about Southern Africa go to:
www.pandg-atlas.com

Map labels:
SUDAN
ETHIOPIA
Lake Turkana
UGANDA
KAMPALA
KENYA
SOMALIA
Kisangani
Kisumu
Equator
ATIC
C
KIGALI
RWANDA
Lake Victoria
NAIROBI
Kilimanjaro 5895m
JUMBURA
BURUNDI
Olduvai Gorge
Mombasa
NGO
Lake Tanganyika
uji-Mayi
DODOMA
Zanzibar
Dar es Salaam
TANZANIA
Kolwezi
Lubumbashi
MALAWI
COMOROS
MORONI
MAYOTTE (to France)
Kitwe
Ndola
Lake Nyasa
LILONGWE
ZAMBIA
SAKA
Zambezi
Blantyre
ctoria Falls
HARARE
ZIMBABWE
MOZAMBIQUE
MADAGASCAR
ANTANANARIVO
MAURITIUS
PORT LOUIS
RÉUNION (to France)
Bulawayo
Beira
TSWANA
Limpopo
Mozambique Channel
BORONE
TSHWANE (PRETORIA)
MBABANE
MAPUTO
Tropic of Capricorn
weto
Johannesburg
SWAZILAND
OEMFONTEIN
MASERU
OTHO
Durban
RICA
DRAKENSBERG
Port Elizabeth
INDIAN OCEAN

N

0 400 800 kilometres
0 400 800 miles

Northern Europe

EUROPE

Norway, Sweden and Denmark are known as Scandinavia. The countries of Estonia, Latvia and Lithuania are called the Baltic States. These six countries, together with Finland and Iceland, are the most northern ones in Europe. During the long, cold winters the Sun rises for only a few hours each day. Most people in Scandinavia live in the cities or towns in the south and around the coast. Throughout Scandinavia there are forests, and many of the trees are used to make furniture and paper. Iron ore is used for making steel, and the water from the lakes and rivers produces electricity in hydroelectric power stations. There are plenty of fish in the coastal waters of northern Europe, and all these countries have strong fishing industries.

Country File

Denmark

Estonia

Finland

Iceland

Latvia

Lithuania

Norway

Sweden

Lapland

The northern part of Norway, Sweden and Finland is known as Lapland. This is the home of the Sami people. They are descended from nomadic people who lived in northern Scandinavia for thousands of years. Some Sami still herd reindeer, which they keep for their milk, meat and skins.

Red squirrel

The red squirrel lives all over northern Europe. Although it is called 'red' it can be black, brown or red with a pale belly. Other mammals, such as brown bears, elk and grey wolves, are also found in the forests of Scandinavia.

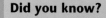

Did you know?

◇ Denmark has some of the longest beaches in the whole of Europe.

◇ Many English words come from Scandinavian languages. The word 'garden' means 'farm' in Danish, and gardens in medieval England used to be full of vegetables!

Two-thirds of the land in Denmark is used for farming. Most of it is used for pig farming or for growing food for the pigs.

Norwegian fjords

Fjords are long, deep, steep-sided valleys, which glaciers carved through the mountains over 150,000 years ago. As the ice melted, the sea levels rose and the valleys flooded with water. Thousands of tourists visit the fjords each year to enjoy the beautiful scenery.

Did you know?

◇ Finland has more than 188,000 lakes and three-quarters of the country is covered by forest.

◇ Norway was rated the world's most peaceful country on the 2007 Global Peace Index.

◇ The national currency of Estonia is called the kroon. It is abbreviated to 'EEK'!

Timber for building

Wood is a very important material for all of the countries in northern Europe. Over the centuries wood has been used for producing fuel, for making furniture and toys and for building houses and churches. There are so many trees in this area that many houses and public buildings are still made from wood today.

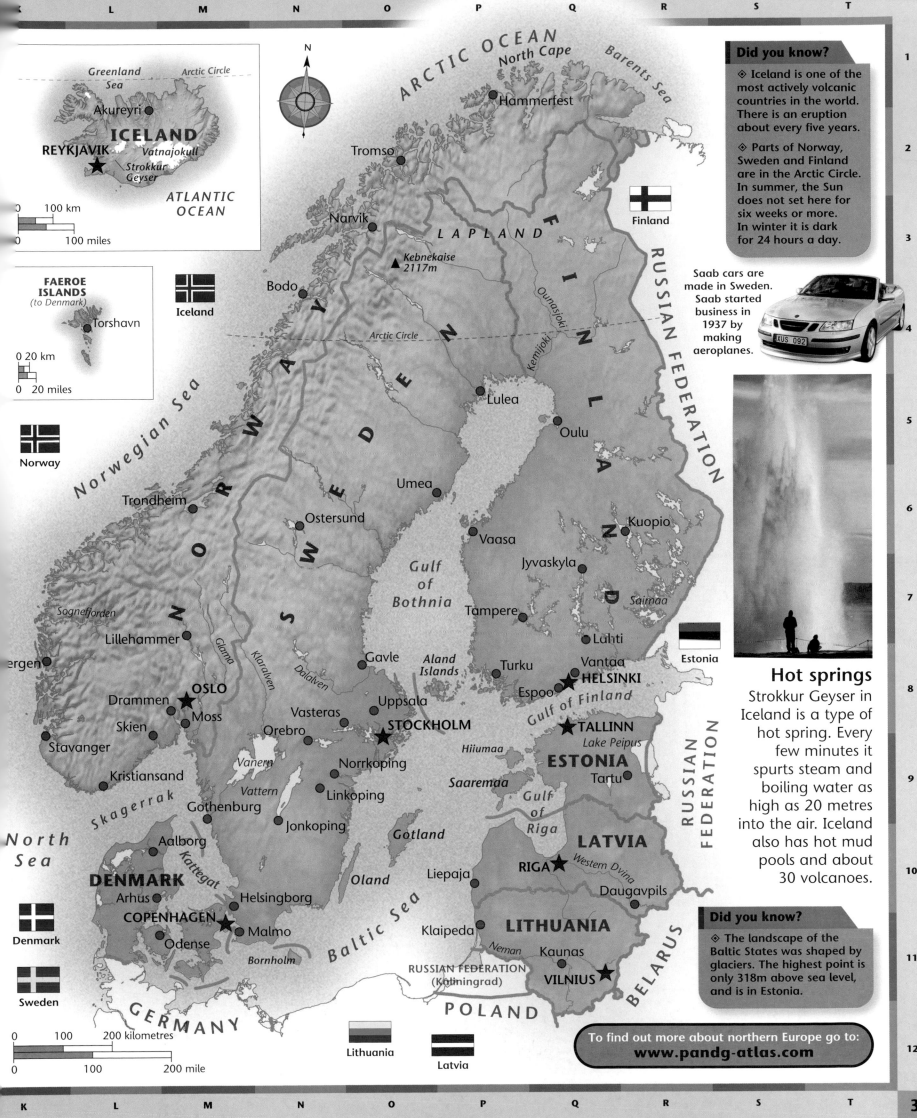

Greenland Sea · Arctic Circle

Akureyri

ICELAND

REYKJAVIK · *Vatnajokull* · *Strokkur Geyser*

ATLANTIC OCEAN

0 — 100 km

0 — 100 miles

FAEROE ISLANDS
(to Denmark)

Torshavn

0 20 km

0 20 miles

Iceland

Norway

Norwegian Sea

ARCTIC OCEAN

North Cape

Barents Sea

Hammerfest

Tromso

LAPLAND

Narvik

▲ Kebnekaise 2117m

Bodo

Ounasjoki

Arctic Circle

Kemijoki

RUSSIAN FEDERATION

Finland

Lulea

Oulu

Umea

Kuopio

Trondheim

Ostersund

Vaasa

Jyvaskyla

Saimaa

Gulf of Bothnia

Tampere

Lahti

Sognefjorden

Lillehammer

Glama

Klaralven

Dalalven

Gavle

Aland Islands

Turku

Vantaa

Estonia

Bergen

OSLO

Drammen

Moss

Skien

Uppsala

HELSINKI

Espoo

Gulf of Finland

Stavanger

Vasteras

Orebro

STOCKHOLM

TALLINN

Hiiumaa

Lake Peipus

Kristiansand

Vanern

Norrkoping

ESTONIA

Tartu

Skagerrak

Vattern

Linkoping

Saaremaa

Gulf of Riga

North Sea

Gothenburg

Jonkoping

Gotland

LATVIA

Aalborg

Kattegat

Oland

RIGA

Western Dvina

Liepaja

DENMARK

Arhus

Helsingborg

Daugavpils

COPENHAGEN

Malmo

Odense

Bornholm

Baltic Sea

Klaipeda

LITHUANIA

Denmark

Neman

Kaunas

Sweden

RUSSIAN FEDERATION
(Kaliningrad)

VILNIUS

BELARUS

GERMANY

POLAND

0 100 200 kilometres

0 100 200 mile

Lithuania

Latvia

N O R W A Y · S W E D E N · F I N L A N D

Saab cars are made in Sweden. Saab started business in 1937 by making aeroplanes.

Hot springs

Strokkur Geyser in Iceland is a type of hot spring. Every few minutes it spurts steam and boiling water as high as 20 metres into the air. Iceland also has hot mud pools and about 30 volcanoes.

To find out more about northern Europe go to:
www.pandg-atlas.com

Western Europe

EUROPE

The area in Europe that is furthest from Asia is known as western Europe. The most northern countries have a mild, wet climate. Further south the climate becomes increasingly warmer. In southern France, Spain and Portugal, the temperature in summer often reaches over 30°C. The land is suitable for many kinds of farming. Oranges are grown in Spain, flowers in the Netherlands and wheat and potatoes are grown throughout western Europe. Many countries also grow grapes to make wine. Wine-making is important in France, Spain and Portugal. Most people in western Europe live in large towns and cities. This region is very popular with holiday-makers, and tourism is a big industry. Electronics and car manufacturing are also major industries in western Europe.

Country File

Andorra

Belgium

France

Ireland

Luxembourg

Monaco

Netherlands

Portugal

Spain

United Kingdom

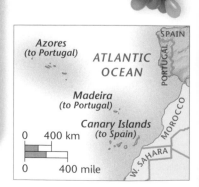

Red fox

Foxes are members of the dog family. They are found all across Europe and survive in towns and cities as well as the countryside. They eat all kinds of things, such as worms, berries, insects, small mammals and household waste.

Did you know?

◇ Three countries in Europe are called principalities, which means that they are reigned over by a prince or princess. They are Andorra, Liechtenstein and Monaco.

The fastest train in the world is the French TGV 'Train à Grande Vitesse', which travels at an average speed of 300km per hour. One TGV reached 574.8km per hour during a test run, which is a world record for a train travelling on ordinary rails.

Did you know?

◇ People in Andorra live the longest lives in the world, at an average of 83.5 years.

◇ People from South America, Indonesia and the Caribbean make up five per cent of the population of the Netherlands. There used to be Dutch colonies in these places.

Costa Brava

The coastal region in northeast Spain known as the Costa Brava stretches for about 160 kilometres along the Mediterranean Sea. It is popular for its sandy beaches and its warm seas. The area is also an important cork-growing region and supplies cork to wine producers all over the world.

Over 500 different varieties of cheese are made in France, including Brie and Roquefort.

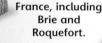

London Eye

Millions of tourists visit London every year for its history, theatres and sights, such as Big Ben and the London Eye. The London Eye is the world's tallest observation wheel, at 135 metres high. About 3.5 million people visit it each year to see the view from the top. Passengers can see for 40 kilometres in all directions.

Did you know?

◇ There are more tomatoes grown in Portugal than any other crop. Over 1 million tonnes of tomatoes are produced every year.

◇ The southern tip of Spain is only 13km from Africa at its closest point.

◇ Belgium is famous for making chocolate and produces 172,000 tonnes of chocolates every year.

Grapes grow on plants called vines, and the areas where wine is produced are called vineyards.

Azores (to Portugal)   SPAIN   ATLANTIC OCEAN   PORTUGAL

Madeira (to Portugal)   MOROCCO

Canary Islands (to Spain)

0   400 km

0   400 mile

W. SAHARA

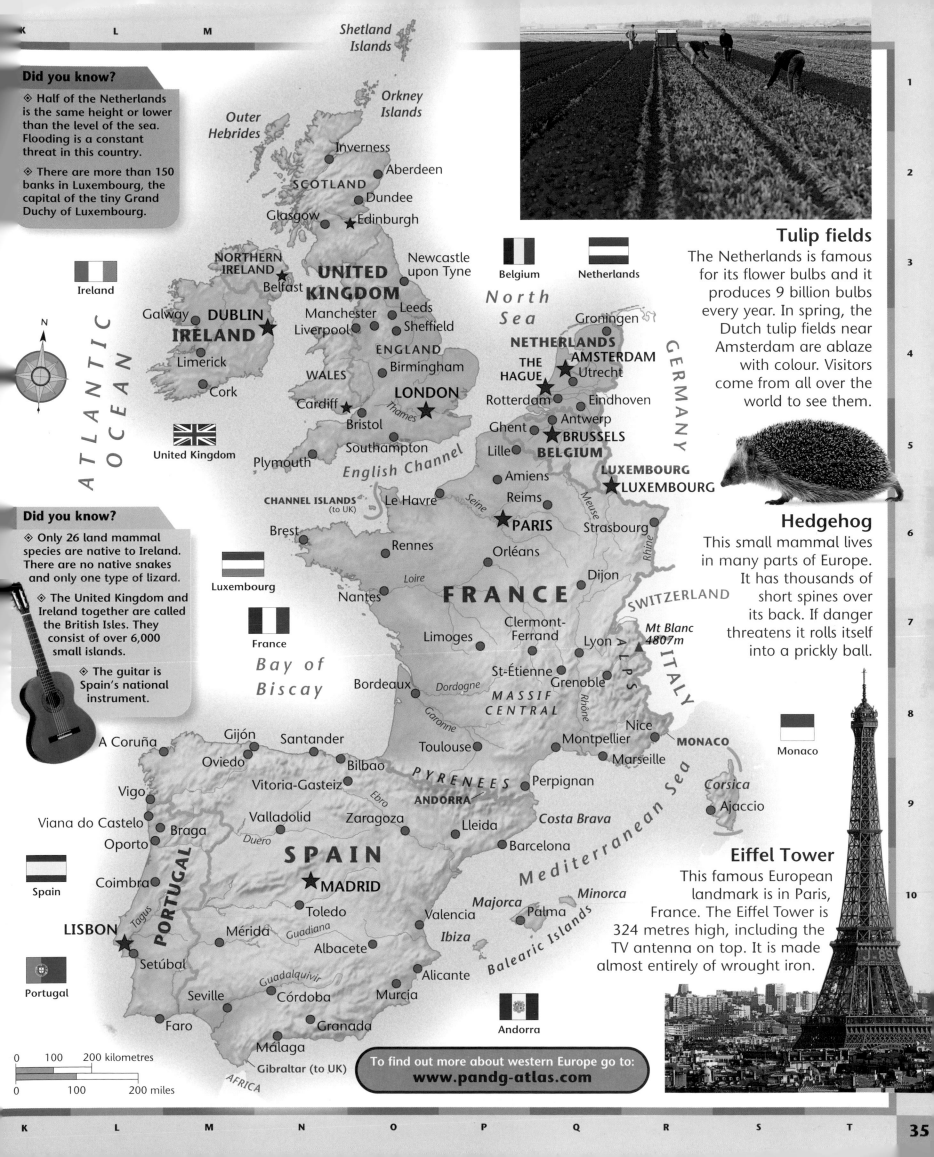

K L M Shetland Islands

1
2
3
4
5
6
7
8
9
10

Did you know?

◇ Half of the Netherlands is the same height or lower than the level of the sea. Flooding is a constant threat in this country.

◇ There are more than 150 banks in Luxembourg, the capital of the tiny Grand Duchy of Luxembourg.

Orkney Islands

Outer Hebrides

Inverness
Aberdeen
SCOTLAND
Dundee
Glasgow
Edinburgh

Ireland

N

A T L A N T I C   O C E A N

NORTHERN IRELAND
Belfast
UNITED KINGDOM
Newcastle upon Tyne

Galway
DUBLIN
IRELAND
Manchester
Leeds
Liverpool
Sheffield

Limerick
ENGLAND
Birmingham
WALES

Cork
Cardiff
LONDON

United Kingdom
Bristol
Thames

Southampton
Plymouth
English Channel

Belgium

Netherlands

North Sea

Groningen

NETHERLANDS
AMSTERDAM
THE HAGUE
Utrecht

Rotterdam
Eindhoven

Ghent
Antwerp

Lille
BRUSSELS
BELGIUM

LUXEMBOURG
LUXEMBOURG

GERMANY

Tulip fields

The Netherlands is famous for its flower bulbs and it produces 9 billion bulbs every year. In spring, the Dutch tulip fields near Amsterdam are ablaze with colour. Visitors come from all over the world to see them.

CHANNEL ISLANDS (to UK)
Le Havre
Amiens
Reims
Strasbourg

Brest
Seine
PARIS
Meuse

Rennes
Orléans
Rhine

Did you know?

◇ Only 26 land mammal species are native to Ireland. There are no native snakes and only one type of lizard.

◇ The United Kingdom and Ireland together are called the British Isles. They consist of over 6,000 small islands.

◇ The guitar is Spain's national instrument.

Luxembourg

France

Loire
Dijon
FRANCE

Nantes

SWITZERLAND

Limoges
Clermont-Ferrand
Lyon
Mt Blanc 4807m

Hedgehog

This small mammal lives in many parts of Europe. It has thousands of short spines over its back. If danger threatens it rolls itself into a prickly ball.

Bay of Biscay

St-Étienne
Grenoble
ITALY

Bordeaux
Dordogne
MASSIF CENTRAL
Rhone

Garonne

Nice
MONACO

A Coruña
Gijón
Santander
Montpellier
Marseille
Monaco

Oviedo
Bilbao
PYRENEES
Perpignan
Corsica

Vigo
Vitoria-Gasteiz
ANDORRA
Ajaccio

Viana do Castelo
Braga
Valladolid
Zaragoza
Lleida
Costa Brava

Oporto
Duero
Barcelona

Spain

SPAIN
MADRID

Eiffel Tower

This famous European landmark is in Paris, France. The Eiffel Tower is 324 metres high, including the TV antenna on top. It is made almost entirely of wrought iron.

Coimbra
PORTUGAL
Toledo
Valencia
Majorca
Minorca

LISBON
Tagus
Mérida
Guadiana
Albacete
Ibiza
Palma

Portugal
Setúbal
Ibiza
Balearic Islands

Guadalquivir
Alicante
Mediterranean Sea

Seville
Córdoba
Murcia

Faro
Granada
Andorra

Málaga
Gibraltar (to UK)
AFRICA

0   100   200 kilometres
0   100   200 miles

To find out more about western Europe go to:
www.pandg-atlas.com

Central Europe

EUROPE

The central part of Europe stretches from the Baltic Sea in the north to the Mediterranean Sea in the south. Winters can be very cold in the north, but the weather gets warmer the further south you go. In Germany and Poland, land is used for mining, industry and farming. People grow crops such as potatoes and barley, and many farmers keep pigs and goats. Further south, especially in Italy, people grow olives, grapes and citrus fruit. Many long rivers run through central Europe, including the Rhine and the Danube. People use these rivers for transporting their goods. A high mountain range called the Alps runs through France, Switzerland, Austria and northern Italy.

Country File

- Austria
- Czech Republic
- Germany
- Italy
- Liechtenstein
- Malta
- Poland
- San Marino
- Slovakia
- Slovenia
- Switzerland
- Vatican City

Alps

This range of mountains is mainly in France, Italy, Switzerland and Austria and is about 1,200 kilometres long. Many people visit the Alps to climb, walk and ski. They are the source of several major European rivers, such as the Rhine, Rhone and Po.

Did you know?

◇ Brown coal (lignite), is central Europe's main fuel and is one of Poland's main exports. It contains lots of sulphur, and burning it to make electricity adds to air pollution and acid rain.

◇ There are lots of different car manufacturers in Italy. Italy has one of the highest number of cars per person in the world.

Lamborghini cars are some of the fastest, most expensive sports cars in the world.

Did you know?

◇ Germany produces enough of the major food products, such as grains, sugar, oils, milk and meat, for its whole population.

Vatican City

The Vatican City is in Rome, Italy. It is the smallest country in the world and it takes up an area of only 440,000 square metres. It contains St Peter's Basilica and the Apostolic Palace, where the pope lives.

Tomatoes and basil are important ingredients in many Italian dishes, including pizza.

Alpine ibex

The ibex is a type of wild goat. It lives high up in the Alps and is sturdy and surefooted. The ibex was hunted almost to extinction in the 19th century but now its numbers are growing.

National parks

There are many national parks in central Europe. This is Triglav National Park in Slovenia. It contains Triglav mountain, which is the highest peak in Slovenia. There are beech and spruce forests, and animals such as chamois and lynx live here.

Did you know?

◇ The highest peak in the Alps is Mont Blanc, on the border of Italy and France. It is 4,807m high.

◇ Pizza and pasta are Italian foods, but they are now enjoyed all over the world.

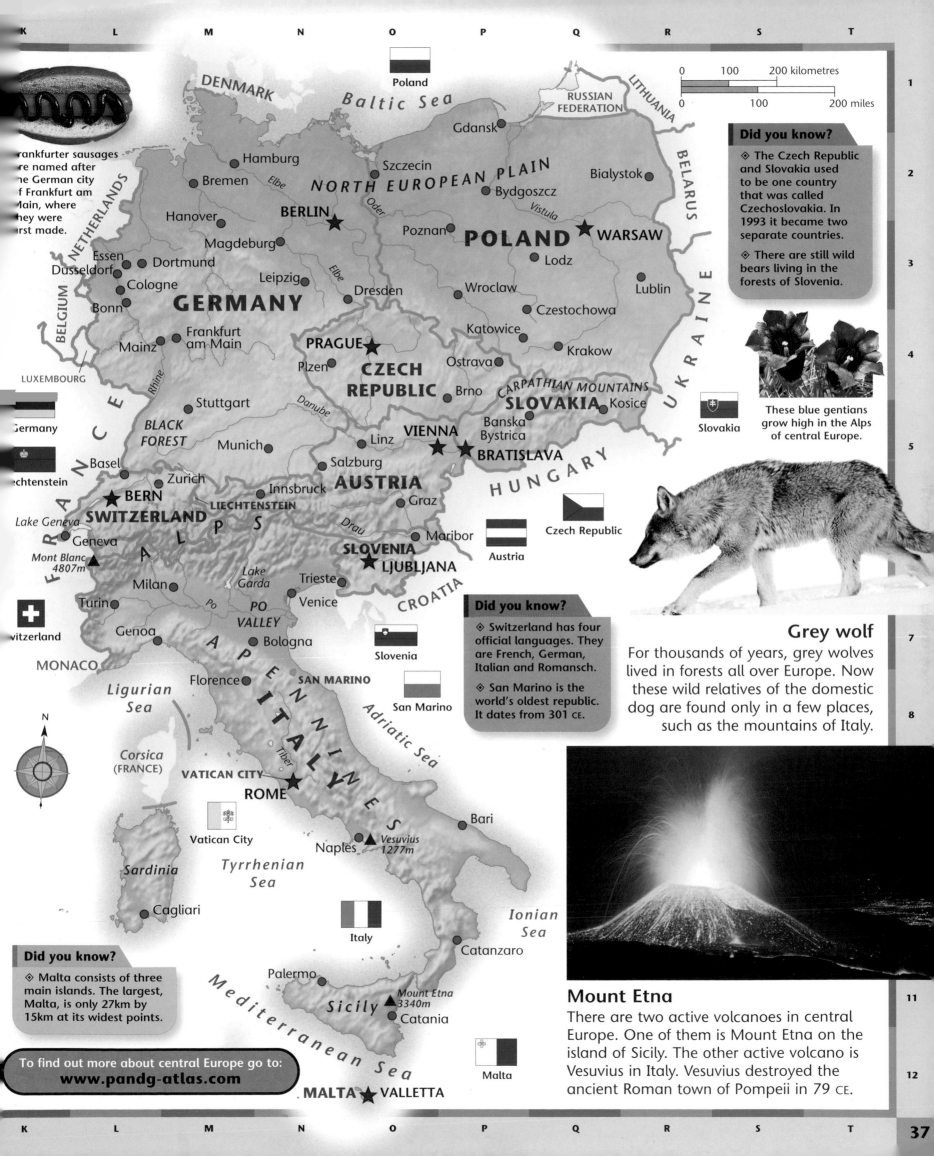

K L M N O P Q R S T

DENMARK

Baltic Sea

RUSSIAN FEDERATION

LITHUANIA

Poland

0   100   200 kilometres

0   100   200 miles

NORTH EUROPEAN PLAIN

Gdansk

Szczecin

Hamburg

Bremen

Elbe

Bialystok

Bydgoszcz

BELARUS

Hanover

BERLIN

Oder

Poznan

POLAND

WARSAW

NETHERLANDS

Magdeburg

Essen

Dortmund

Leipzig

Lodz

Dusseldorf

Cologne

Elbe

Dresden

Wroclaw

Lublin

Bonn

GERMANY

Czestochowa

BELGIUM

Katowice

UKRAINE

Frankfurt am Main

Mainz

Rhine

PRAGUE

Krakow

LUXEMBOURG

CZECH REPUBLIC

Plzen

Ostrava

Germany

Stuttgart

Danube

Brno

CARPATHIAN MOUNTAINS

SLOVAKIA

Kosice

Slovakia

These blue gentians grow high in the Alps of central Europe.

Liechtenstein

BLACK FOREST

Munich

Banska Bystrica

VIENNA

Linz

Basel

Zurich

Salzburg

AUSTRIA

BRATISLAVA

HUNGARY

BERN

Innsbruck

SWITZERLAND

LIECHTENSTEIN

Graz

Lake Geneva

A L P S

Drau

Maribor

Czech Republic

Geneva

Mont Blanc 4807m

SLOVENIA

LJUBLJANA

Austria

FRANCE

Milan

Lake Garda

Trieste

Switzerland

Turin

Po

PO VALLEY

Venice

CROATIA

Genoa

Bologna

Grey wolf

MONACO

A P E N N I N E S

Slovenia

For thousands of years, grey wolves lived in forests all over Europe. Now these wild relatives of the domestic dog are found only in a few places, such as the mountains of Italy.

Ligurian Sea

Florence

SAN MARINO

San Marino

Corsica (FRANCE)

I T A L Y

Adriatic Sea

N

VATICAN CITY

ROME

Tiber

Vatican City

Bari

Vesuvius 1277m

Naples

Sardinia

Tyrrhenian Sea

Ionian Sea

Cagliari

Italy

Catanzaro

Palermo

Sicily

Mount Etna 3340m

Catania

Mount Etna

There are two active volcanoes in central Europe. One of them is Mount Etna on the island of Sicily. The other active volcano is Vesuvius in Italy. Vesuvius destroyed the ancient Roman town of Pompeii in 79 CE.

Mediterranean Sea

Malta

To find out more about central Europe go to:
www.pandg-atlas.com

MALTA VALLETTA

K L M N O P Q R S T

Southeast Europe

EUROPE

Much of this area is mountainous, although there are fertile, flat areas in the north and east. Farming is important in these countries and many crops, such as grapes, tobacco, roses and wheat, are grown. In the north, the winters are very cold. Further south and around the coast, winters are milder and summers are hot and dry. During the past 30 years there have been many changes and wars in southeast Europe, caused by political, ethnic and religious problems. In the 1990s, Ukraine, Belarus and Moldova gained independence from the former Soviet Union. The former Yugoslavia split into the republics of Croatia, Serbia, Bosnia and Herzegovina, Macedonia and Montenegro. After years of war, some areas are still recovering from their problems.

Country File

Albania

Belarus

Bosnia and Herzegovina

Bulgaria

Croatia

Greece

Hungary

Macedonia

Moldova

Montenegro

Romania

Serbia

Ukraine

Most of the world's rose oil is produced in Bulgaria. Rose oil is used in luxury perfumes, soaps and cosmetics and is more valuable than gold.

Did you know?

◇ The percentage of people who smoke cigarettes is higher in Romania than in any other European country.

◇ Some of the water from the springs in Budapest is over 90°C. It has to be mixed with cold water before it can be used.

Dubrovnik

The town of Dubrovnik in Croatia is encircled by 1,940 metres of city walls, which were built over 400 years ago. There are several towers and fortresses along the walls, making it one of the strongest fortifications in Europe.

Did you know?

◇ The huge Lake Prespa has an area of 274 sq km. Most of it is in Macedonia, but some is in Albania and some in Greece. It is fed by underground streams and is linked by underground channels to Lake Ohrid. This even bigger lake, which is 358 sq km, is shared by Macedonia and Albania.

Budapest

The Hungarian city of Budapest sits on a geological fault line. There are more than 120 springs in the city, where hot water rises naturally from the ground. People have built spas and baths over the hot springs for almost 2,000 years.

Wild boar

There are wild boar roaming freely throughout the forests of southeast Europe. These nocturnal animals forage for food from dusk until dawn. They live in groups called 'sounders', containing about 20 animals. The groups are made up of three or four females and their young.

Olives have been grown in Greece for over 2,000 years, and olives and olive oil are major exports. Olives are also important ingredients in many dishes, including Greek salads.

Acropolis

Athens, the capital of Greece, is named after Athena, the goddess of war in Greek mythology. The Parthenon is Athena's chief temple. It was built in the 5th century BCE on the Acropolis hill above Athens. Acropolis means 'edge of the city'.

Ukraine

The rich dark soil of Ukraine is ideal for farming. Formerly part of the Soviet Union, Ukraine used to be known as 'the bread basket of Russia'. Today it exports large amounts of grain, vegetables, dairy produce, meat and sunflower seeds.

Much of the soil in Moldova is rich and fertile. Many vegetables are grown there, but grapes and sunflowers are the most important crops.

Belarus

Ukraine

Bosnia and Herzegovina

Hungary

Croatia

Serbia

Montenegro

Albania

Moldova

Romania

Bulgaria

Macedonia

Greece

Pine marten

These animals are related to weasels and are about the size of a domestic cat. They live in wooded areas all over Europe and spend a lot of their time in trees, where they build their dens. Pine martens feed mostly on small mammals, birds, frogs, insects and carrion.

0 100 200 kilometres

0 100 200 miles

To find out more about southeast Europe go to: **www.pandg-atlas.com**

Map labels

LITHUANIA · LATVIA · RUSSIAN FEDERATION

Vitsyebsk · **BELARUS** · **MINSK** · Mahilyow · Hrodna · Babruysk · Homyel' · Brest · *Pripet Marshes* · *Pripet* · *Dnieper* · Chernihiv · Chernobyl' · **KIEV** · Luts'k · Zhytomyr · Kharkiv · Donets · **U K R A I N E** · Poltava · Luhans'k · Cherkasy · Dnipropetrovs'k · L'viv · Ivano-Frankivs'k · Kirovohrad · *Dnieper* · Donets'k · Chernivtsi · *Dniester* · Kryvyy Rih · Zaporizhzhya · *Southern Bug* · **MOLDOVA** · Mariupol' · Iasi · *Prut* · **CHISINAU** · Mykolayiv · *BLACK SEA LOWLAND* · *Sea of Azov*

POLAND · SLOVAKIA · *CARPATHIAN MOUNTAINS* · Bacau · Tiraspol' · Odesa · *Crimea* · Simferopol'

AUSTRIA · Gyor · Miskolc · *Tisza* · Nyiregyhaza · **BUDAPEST** · Debrecen · **HUNGARY** · Cluj-Napoca · *Transylvania* · Pecs · *Drava* · Szeged · **ROMANIA** · Brasov · Galati · *Black Sea*

SLOVENIA · **ZAGREB** · Osijek · *Sava* · Novi Sad · Timisoara · TRANSYLVANIAN ALPS · Ploiesti · Braila · Rijeka · **CROATIA** · Banja Luka · Tuzla · **BOSNIA & HERZEGOVINA** · **BELGRADE** · **BUCHAREST** · Zadar · *Dalmatia* · **SARAJEVO** · Craiova · Constanta · Split · Mostar · **SERBIA** · *Danube* · Ruse · Dubrovnik · *Adriatic Sea* · Nis · Montana · **BULGARIA** · **MONTENEGRO** · **PRISTINA** · *BALKAN MOUNTAINS* · Varna · **PODGORICA** · **KOSOVO** · **SOFIA** · Sliven · Burgas · Shkoder · *RHODOPE* · Musala 2925m · Plovdiv · (only partially recognized) · **SKOPJE** · *MOUNTAINS* · Durres · **MACEDONIA** · Komotini · **TIRANA** · *Lake Ohrid* · Bitola · *Lake Prespa* · Kavala · TURKEY · **ALBANIA** · Salonica

Kerkyra · *PINDOS MOUNTAINS* · Larisa · *Aegean* · *Lesbos Sea* · *Corfu* · Arta · **GREECE** · Lamia · *Ionian Sea* · Patra · **ATHENS** · Piraeus · *Peloponnese* · *Cyclades* · *Dodecanese* · TURKEY · *Mediterranean Sea* · *Sea of Crete* · *Rhodes* · Irakleio · *Crete*

N

Russian Federation

EUROPE AND ASIA

The Russian Federation is the largest country in the world and it stretches across two continents. The area to the west of the Ural Mountains is in Europe, and the area to the east is in Asia. Russia's climate varies massively, from Arctic weather in the north to mild weather in the south. More than three-quarters of the country is occupied by Siberia, but less than 30 per cent of the population lives there because the region has such long, cold winters. Siberia contains huge deposits of oil and natural gas. Russia also has fertile farmland and rich mineral deposits. Its main exports are oil and oil products, natural gas, metals, wood and wood products. Most of the people there are Russians, but there are more than 120 other ethnic groups with many different religions, languages and cultures.

Country File

Russian Federation

Russian Federation

Franz Josef Land

NORWAY
FINLAND
Murmansk
KOLA PENINSULA
Arctic Circle
White Sea
Barents Sea
Novaya Zemlya
Kara Sea
YAMAL PENINSULA

KALININGRAD (to Russia)
Kaliningrad
ESTONIA
LATVIA
LITH.
POLAND
BELARUS
Lake Ladoga
Petrozavodsk
St Petersburg
Velikiy Novgorod
Lake Onega
Archangel
Northern Dvina
Pechora
Vorkuta

Tver'
NORTH EUROPEAN PLAIN
Syktyvkar
Ob'

MOSCOW ★
Yaroslavl'
Tula
Ryazan'
Nizhniy Novgorod
Kirov
Perm'
WEST SIBERIAN PLAIN

UKRAINE
Don
CENTRAL RUSSIAN UPLAND
Voronezh
Kazan'
Izhevsk
Penza
Ul'yanovsk
URAL MOUNTAINS
R U S
Ob'

Rostov-na-Donu
Saratov
Volga
Samara
Ufa
Yekaterinburg
Trans-Siberian Railway
Tyumen
Irtysh

Volgograd
Krasnodar
Stavropol'
Orenburg
Chelyabinsk
Omsk
Tomsk

El'brus 5642m
CAUCASUS
Astrakhan'
Novosibirsk
Ob'

GEORGIA
Groznyy
Caspian Sea
KAZAKHSTAN
Kemerovo
Barnaul
Novokuznetsk

AZERBAIJAN

St Basil's Cathedral

St Basil's in Moscow is one of the most famous buildings in the world. It was built in Red Square by Tsar Ivan IV 'the Terrible' and was finished in 1560, after five years of building. It is actually eight separate churches, joined together with a central tower.

Did you know?

◇ Lake Baikal is the deepest lake in the world, at up to 1,620m deep. It is also the oldest freshwater lake.

◇ Russia has two great classical ballet companies, called the Bolshoi and Mariinsky (formerly called the Kirov), which are both famous in many parts of the world.

Siberian tiger

The Siberian tiger is in danger of extinction. Its habitat is being destroyed and it is hunted for its body parts, which are used in traditional Chinese medicine. There are only about 500 left in the wild.

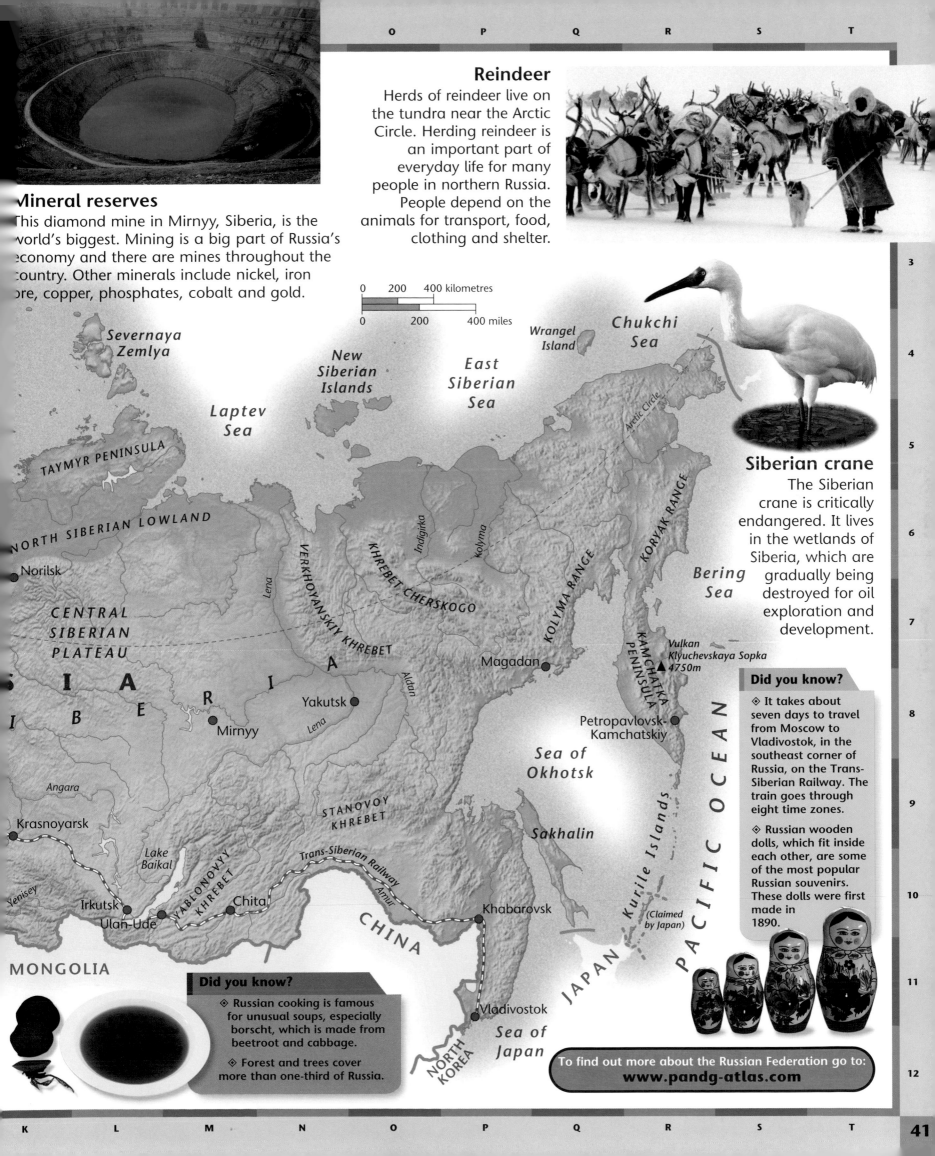

Mineral reserves

This diamond mine in Mirnyy, Siberia, is the world's biggest. Mining is a big part of Russia's economy and there are mines throughout the country. Other minerals include nickel, iron ore, copper, phosphates, cobalt and gold.

Reindeer

Herds of reindeer live on the tundra near the Arctic Circle. Herding reindeer is an important part of everyday life for many people in northern Russia. People depend on the animals for transport, food, clothing and shelter.

Siberian crane

The Siberian crane is critically endangered. It lives in the wetlands of Siberia, which are gradually being destroyed for oil exploration and development.

0 200 400 kilometres

0 200 400 miles

Map labels:

Severnaya Zemlya
New Siberian Islands
East Siberian Sea
Wrangel Island
Chukchi Sea
Laptev Sea
TAYMYR PENINSULA
NORTH SIBERIAN LOWLAND
Norilsk
CENTRAL SIBERIAN PLATEAU
SIBERIA
Mirnyy
Yakutsk
Lena
Angara
Krasnoyarsk
Yenisey
Irkutsk
Ulan-Ude
Lake Baikal
YABLONOVYY KHREBET
Chita
Trans-Siberian Railway
Amur
CHINA
MONGOLIA
VERKHOYANSKIY KHREBET
KHREBET CHERSKOGO
Indigirka
Kolyma
Aldan
Lena
STANOVOY KHREBET
KOLYMA RANGE
KORYAK RANGE
Arctic Circle
Magadan
Bering Sea
KAMCHATKA PENINSULA
Vulkan Klyuchevskaya Sopka 4750m
Petropavlovsk-Kamchatskiy
Sea of Okhotsk
Sakhalin
Khabarovsk
Vladivostok
NORTH KOREA
Sea of Japan
JAPAN
Kurile Islands
(Claimed by Japan)
PACIFIC OCEAN

Did you know?

◇ Russian cooking is famous for unusual soups, especially borscht, which is made from beetroot and cabbage.

◇ Forest and trees cover more than one-third of Russia.

Did you know?

◇ It takes about seven days to travel from Moscow to Vladivostok, in the southeast corner of Russia, on the Trans-Siberian Railway. The train goes through eight time zones.

◇ Russian wooden dolls, which fit inside each other, are some of the most popular Russian souvenirs. These dolls were first made in 1890.

To find out more about the Russian Federation go to:
www.pandg-atlas.com

3 4 5 6 7 8 9 10 11 12

Southwest Asia

ASIA

Country File

- Armenia
- Azerbaijan
- Bahrain
- Cyprus
- Georgia
- Iran
- Iraq
- Israel
- Jordan
- Kuwait
- Lebanon
- Oman
- Qatar
- Saudi Arabia
- Syria
- Turkey
- United Arab Emirates
- Yemen

Almost all of Southwest Asia is desert. Temperatures can soar to over 30°C in the summer and very little rain falls. Although the weather is hot and dry, people have lived here, in cities and towns, for over 7,000 years. Three of the world's most important religions started here: Christianity, Islam and Judaism. This area has suffered wars for many thousands of years and the conflicts still continue. Most of the wars are about land ownership or disagreements about religion. The biggest source of income for many of these countries is from oil and gas. Oil has made some countries, such as the Arab states, very rich. Tourism is an important industry in several countries, including Turkey and Israel. Turkey and Iran are famous for carpets, which are exported around the world.

Cyprus

BULGARI

Istan

Bu

GREECE

TURKISH REPUBLI
NORTHERN CYI
(recognized only by Tu

Syria

Me

Lebanon

Mecca

The Ka'bah, a shrine inside the Sacred Mosque in Mecca in Saudi Arabia, is regarded by Muslims as the most sacred place on Earth. All able-bodied Muslims who can afford to are meant to make a pilgrimage there at least once in their lifetime.

Aubergines, apricots pistachios and walnuts are important crops in this area.

Petra

The ancient city of Petra in Jordan lies deep inside a desert gorge. Most of the buildings were carved out of solid rock. Once, this ruined city was the capital of an Arab kingdom. Now it is a popular tourist attraction.

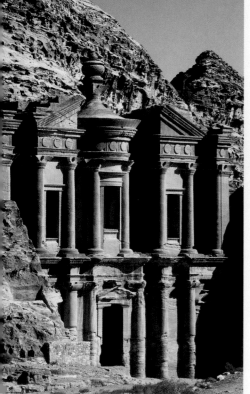

Did you know?

◈ The lowest land on Earth that is not covered by ice is next to the Dead Sea. The shores of this lake are almost 400m below sea level.

◈ Turkey is one of the few countries in the world that produces enough food for all its people. Half of the land in Turkey is used for agriculture (farming).

Arabian oryx

The Arabian oryx was hunted to extinction in the wild. Then, after a worldwide breeding programme in zoos, it was re-introduced into the wild in Oman. Today there are two herds of oryx roaming freely.

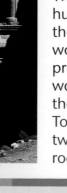

Dubai

The Burj al-Arab hotel in Dubai in the United Arab Emirates was the tallest hotel in the world when it opened in 1999. It is 321 metres high and has a helicopter pad on the 28th floor. The hotel stands on an artificial island and it was designed to look like a big sail.

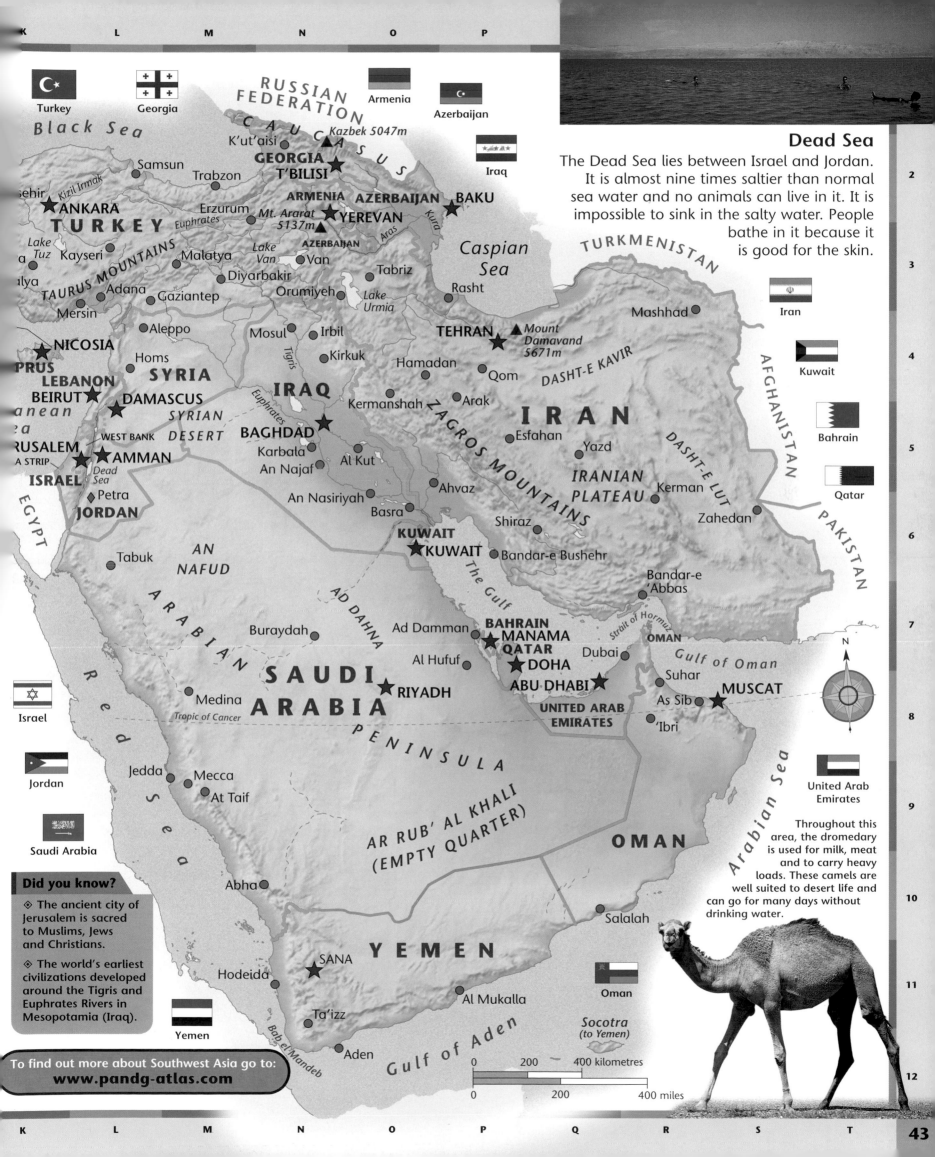

Turkey Georgia Armenia Azerbaijan Iraq

Black Sea
RUSSIAN FEDERATION
CAUCASUS
Kazbek 5047m
K'ut'aisi
GEORGIA T'BILISI
Samsun
Trabzon
...ehir Kizil Irmak
ANKARA
TURKEY Euphrates
Erzurum
Mt. Ararat 5137m
ARMENIA AZERBAIJAN BAKU
YEREVAN
AZERBAIJAN
Aras Kura
Caspian Sea
TURKMENISTAN
Lake Tuz Kayseri
Malatya
Lake Van Van
Tabriz
Mashhad
Iran
...lya Diyarbakir
Orumiyeh
Lake Urmia
Rasht
TAURUS MOUNTAINS
Adana Gaziantep
Aleppo
Mosul Irbil
TEHRAN Mount Damavand 5671m
DASHT-E KAVIR
AFGHANISTAN
Mersin
NICOSIA
Homs SYRIA
Tigris Kirkuk
Hamadan
Qom
Kuwait
PRUS LEBANON
IRAQ
Kermanshah Arak
I R A N
Kuwait
BEIRUT DAMASCUS
SYRIAN DESERT
Euphrates
BAGHDAD
Esfahan Yazd
IRANIAN PLATEAU
DASHT-E LUT
Bahrain
...anean ...a
WEST BANK
Karbala
An Najaf
Al Kut
ZAGROS MOUNTAINS
Kerman
Bahrain
RUSALEM AMMAN
An Nasiriyah
Ahvaz
Zahedan
Qatar
A STRIP Dead Sea
Basra
Shiraz
PAKISTAN
ISRAEL
Petra
An Nasiriyah
Qatar
EGYPT JORDAN
KUWAIT KUWAIT
Bandar-e Bushehr
Israel
Tabuk
AN NAFUD
The Gulf
Bandar-e 'Abbas
AD DAHNA
BAHRAIN MANAMA
OMAN
N
Buraydah
Ad Damman QATAR DOHA
Dubai
Strait of Hormuz
Gulf of Oman
Al Hufuf ABU DHABI
Suhar
Israel
S A U D I
RIYADH
UNITED ARAB EMIRATES
MUSCAT
Medina
As Sib
'Ibri
Arabian Sea
Jordan
A R A B I A
Tropic of Cancer
PENINSULA
Jedda Mecca
At Taif
United Arab Emirates
Saudi Arabia
AR RUB' AL KHALI (EMPTY QUARTER)
OMAN
Abha
Salalah
Red Sea
SANA
Oman
Y E M E N
Hodeida
Al Mukalla
Ta'izz
Socotra (to Yemen)
Yemen
Bab el Mandeb
Aden
Gulf of Aden

Dead Sea

The Dead Sea lies between Israel and Jordan. It is almost nine times saltier than normal sea water and no animals can live in it. It is impossible to sink in the salty water. People bathe in it because it is good for the skin.

Throughout this area, the dromedary is used for milk, meat and to carry heavy loads. These camels are well suited to desert life and can go for many days without drinking water.

Did you know?

◇ The ancient city of Jerusalem is sacred to Muslims, Jews and Christians.

◇ The world's earliest civilizations developed around the Tigris and Euphrates Rivers in Mesopotamia (Iraq).

To find out more about Southwest Asia go to:
www.pandg-atlas.com

0 200 400 kilometres
0 200 400 miles

Central Asia

ASIA

The Pamirs, in the southeast of this region, form the second highest mountain range in the world (the Himalayas are the highest). Mountains also cover most of Kyrgyzstan and Tajikistan and much of Afghanistan. Kazakhstan has open grasslands, and further south in Uzbekistan and Turkmenistan there is a lot of sandy desert. Central Asia is land-locked, which means that it is cut off from the sea, although it has a huge inland lake called the Caspian Sea. This area gets very little rain and winters and summers have extreme temperatures. There are few large cities and most people live in rural areas. Most of the farming is around the fertile river valleys at the base of the mountains and in Kazakhstan. The main crops include cotton, peaches, melons and apricots. Central Asia has large deposits of oil, coal and natural gas and minerals such as iron and copper. Industries are mostly traditional ones, and some areas specialize in making carpets and leather goods.

Country File

Afghanistan

Kazakhstan

Kyrgyzstan

Tajikistan

Turkmenistan

Uzbekistan

Did you know?

◇ The belt of grassland that stretches across Kazakhstan is called the steppes, which is the Russian word for grassland.

◇ There are huge reserves of coal in Central Asia. It is used mostly to fuel power stations.

RUSSIAN FEDERATION

Ural'sk

Caspian Depressio

Atyrau

Aktau

Caspian Sea

Turkmenbasy

Balkanabat

Did you know?

◇ The Caspian Sea, in the west, is the largest saltwater lake in the world. It takes up an area of 371,000 sq km. This massive lake is bordered by five countries – Russia, Kazakhstan, Iran, Turkmenistan and Azerbaijan.

Aral Sea

The Aral Sea once covered 68,000 square kilometres. But since 1960, it has shrunk to a quarter of its size because water from rivers that flow into the lake is being diverted to use for irrigation. Old ships that used to float on the lake are now sitting on dry land.

Samarqand

One of the oldest cities in Central Asia is Samarqand, which contains some of the finest buildings in this area. They include several Islamic schools called madrasahs. Shirdar madrasah, shown here, was built in the early 1600s. It is decorated with millions of tiles.

Snow leopard

The snow leopard lives high in the mountains of Central Asia. This big cat has very thick fur, which can be up to 10 centimetres long in places.

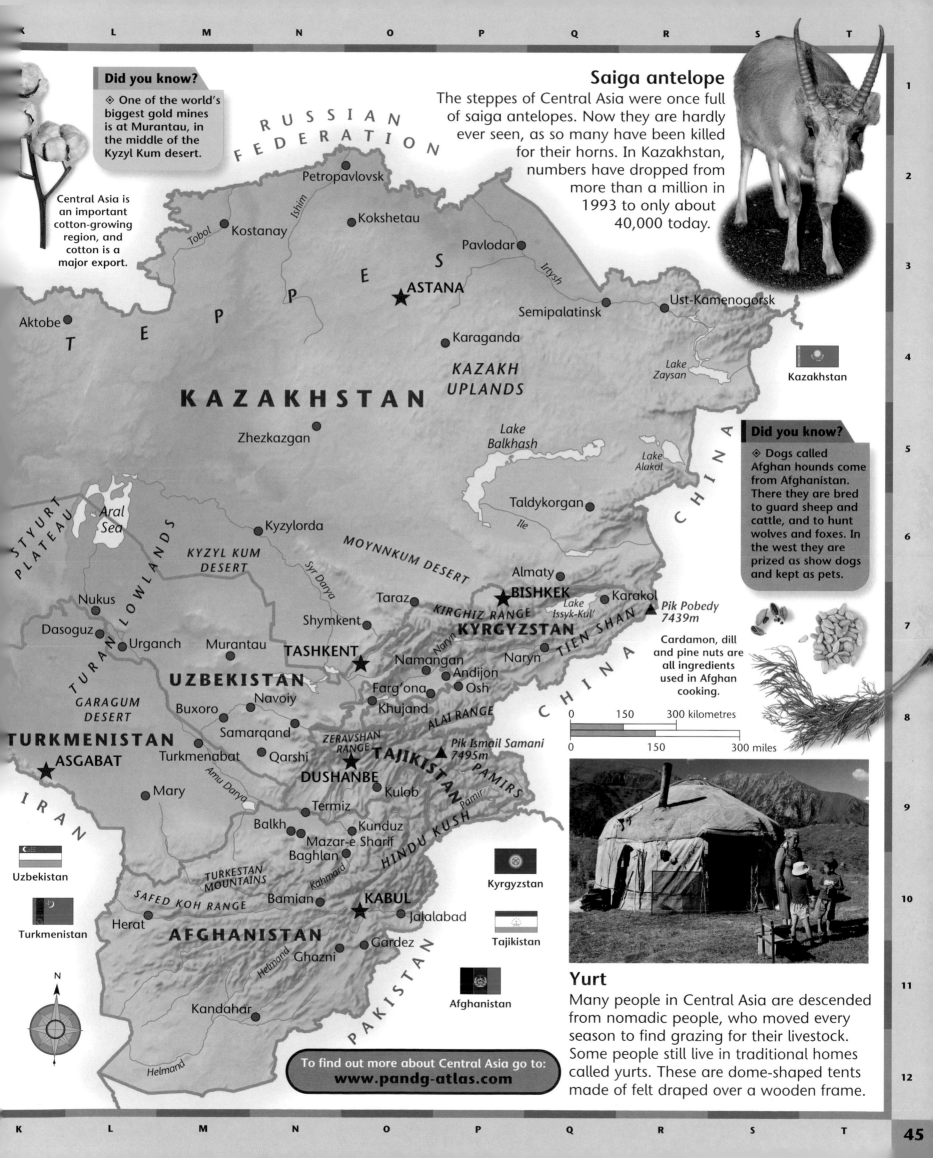

Saiga antelope

The steppes of Central Asia were once full of saiga antelopes. Now they are hardly ever seen, as so many have been killed for their horns. In Kazakhstan, numbers have dropped from more than a million in 1993 to only about 40,000 today.

Did you know?

◈ One of the world's biggest gold mines is at Murantau, in the middle of the Kyzyl Kum desert.

Central Asia is an important cotton-growing region, and cotton is a major export.

Did you know?

◈ Dogs called Afghan hounds come from Afghanistan. There they are bred to guard sheep and cattle, and to hunt wolves and foxes. In the west they are prized as show dogs and kept as pets.

Cardamon, dill and pine nuts are all ingredients used in Afghan cooking.

RUSSIAN FEDERATION

Petropavlovsk

Ishim

Tobol

Kostanay

Kokshetau

Pavlodar

Irtysh

ASTANA

Ust-Kamenogorsk

Semipalatinsk

Aktobe

Karaganda

T E P P E S

Lake Zaysan

Kazakhstan

KAZAKH UPLANDS

K A Z A K H S T A N

Zhezkazgan

Lake Balkhash

Lake Alakol

STYURT PLATEAU

Aral Sea

Kyzylorda

MOYNNKUM DESERT

Taldykorgan

Ile

CHINA

KYZYL KUM DESERT

TURAN LOWLANDS

Nukus

Syr Darya

Almaty

Taraz

BISHKEK

Karakol

Dasoguz

Urganch

Murantau

Shymkent

KIRGHIZ RANGE

Lake 'Issyk-Kul'

Pik Pobedy 7439m

Namangan

KYRGYZSTAN

Naryn

TIEN SHAN

TASHKENT

Naryn

Andijon

UZBEKISTAN

Farg'ona

Osh

Buxoro

Navoiy

Khujand

ALAI RANGE

C H I N A

GARAGUM DESERT

Samarqand

ZERAVSHAN RANGE

Pik Ismail Samani 7495m

0   150   300 kilometres

0   150   300 miles

TURKMENISTAN

Turkmenabat

Qarshi

TAJIKISTAN

PAMIRS

ASGABAT

DUSHANBE

Kulob

Pamir

Mary

Amu Darya

Termiz

Kunduz

I R A N

Balkh

Mazar-e Sharif

Baghlan

HINDU KUSH

Uzbekistan

TURKESTAN MOUNTAINS

Kahmard

Kyrgyzstan

Turkmenistan

SAFED KOH RANGE

Bamian

KABUL

Herat

Jalalabad

Tajikistan

AFGHANISTAN

Gardez

Ghazni

Helmand

Afghanistan

PAKISTAN

Kandahar

N

To find out more about Central Asia go to:
www.pandg-atlas.com

Helmand

Yurt

Many people in Central Asia are descended from nomadic people, who moved every season to find grazing for their livestock. Some people still live in traditional homes called yurts. These are dome-shaped tents made of felt draped over a wooden frame.

South Asia
ASIA

This area is also called the Indian subcontinent. South Asia is separated from the rest of Asia by the towering peaks of the Himalayas. The tops of these mountains are always covered in snow. In the south there are lush tropical rainforests, and in the west are huge areas of desert. India has a typical monsoon climate. From March to June it is hot and dry. The wet season is from June to September, when large amounts of rain fall, often causing floods. October to February is cool and dry. Over one-fifth of the world's population lives in this area. After centuries of invasion and occupation, people have a rich variety of cultures and religions and thousands of languages are spoken. Nearly two-thirds of the population work in agriculture, although most farmers grow only enough for their family. Rice grows in the wetter areas of the east and west, and millet and corn grow on higher areas inland. Tea is an important crop, especially in southwest India and Sri Lanka.

Country File
Bangladesh

Bhutan

India

Maldives

Nepal

Pakistan

Sri Lanka

The population of India is the second biggest in the world (China has the largest population). There are now about 1,130 million people living in India.

Pakistan

IRAN

CENTRAL M RANG

Did you know?
◈ Bangladesh is one of the most densely populated countries in the world and its population is one of the poorest. Most people survive by growing their own food.

◈ There are over 270 species of snake in India, including about 50 venomous ones, such as this king cobra.

A cobra rears up and spreads its hood when it is alarmed.

Bollywood
Film making in India is a huge industry and it is known as 'Bollywood'. The films often contain spectacular song-and-dance routines, with expert fight scenes and beautiful heroes and heroines. Bollywood is based in the city of Mumbai, which used to be called Bombay.

Did you know?
◈ Over 200 people have died trying to climb Mt Everest, and every year this number is rising.

◈ The River Ganges is sacred to people who follow the Hindu religion and it is worshipped as a goddess.

◈ About 800 films are made every year in Bollywood.

Taj Mahal
The Mughal emperor Shah Jahan built the beautiful Taj Mahal in Agra, India, in memory of his favourite wife, Mumtaz Mahal. It took 22 years to build and was finished in 1648. The Taj Mahal consists of four buildings, one of which is a tomb containing the bodies of Shah Jahan and his wife.

Tea plantations
Sri Lanka and parts of India have the ideal climate for tea growing. Only the youngest tea leaves are picked. These are then wilted, oxidized, rolled and dried to produce the tea that we use to make the popular drink.

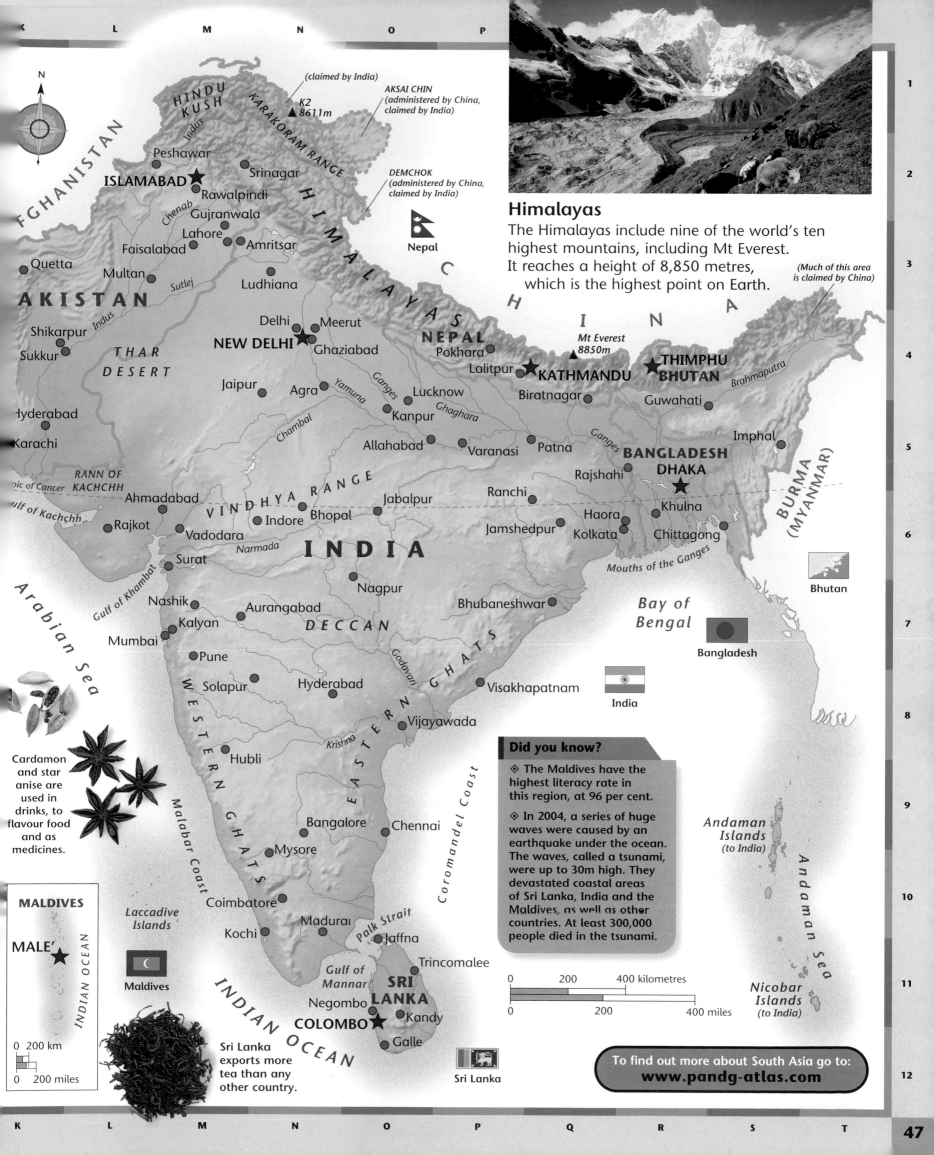

Himalayas

The Himalayas include nine of the world's ten highest mountains, including Mt Everest. It reaches a height of 8,850 metres, which is the highest point on Earth.

(Much of this area is claimed by China)

AFGHANISTAN

HINDU KUSH

KARAKORAM RANGE

(claimed by India)

K2 ▲ 8611m

AKSAI CHIN *(administered by China, claimed by India)*

DEMCHOK *(administered by China, claimed by India)*

Peshawar

ISLAMABAD ★

Srinagar

Rawalpindi

Indus

Chenab

Gujranwala

Lahore

Faisalabad

Amritsar

Quetta

Multan

Sutlej

Ludhiana

AKISTAN

H I M A L A Y A S

Nepal

C   H   I   N   A

Shikarpur

Indus

THAR DESERT

Delhi

Meerut

NEW DELHI ★

Ghaziabad

NEPAL

Pokhara

Lalitpur

★ **KATHMANDU**

Mt Everest ▲ 8850m

★ **THIMPHU**
BHUTAN

Sukkur

Jaipur

Agra

Yamuna

Ganges

Lucknow

Biratnagar

Guwahati

Brahmaputra

Hyderabad

Karachi

Chambal

Ghaghara

Kanpur

Allahabad

Varanasi

Patna

Ganges

BANGLADESH
DHAKA ★

Imphal

RANN OF KACHCHH

pic of Cancer

Gulf of Kachchh

Ahmadabad

V I N D H Y A   R A N G E

Jabalpur

Ranchi

Rajshahi

Khulna

BURMA (MYANMAR)

Rajkot

Indore

Bhopal

Jamshedpur

Haora

Kolkata

Chittagong

Vadodara

Narmada

I N D I A

Gulf of Khambat

Surat

Nagpur

Bhubaneshwar

Mouths of the Ganges

Bhutan

Nashik

Aurangabad

D E C C A N

Bay of Bengal

Kalyan

Mumbai

Pune

E A S T E R N   G H A T S

W E S T E R N   G H A T S

Solapur

Hyderabad

Godavari

Visakhapatnam

Bangladesh

India

Vijayawada

Krishna

Hubli

Did you know?

◊ The Maldives have the highest literacy rate in this region, at 96 per cent.

◊ In 2004, a series of huge waves were caused by an earthquake under the ocean. The waves, called a tsunami, were up to 30m high. They devastated coastal areas of Sri Lanka, India and the Maldives, as well as other countries. At least 300,000 people died in the tsunami.

Cardamon and star anise are used in drinks, to flavour food and as medicines.

Bangalore

Chennai

Coromandel Coast

Mysore

Andaman Islands (to India)

Andaman Sea

Malabar Coast

Coimbatore

Laccadive Islands

Madurai

Palk Strait

Kochi

Jaffna

Trincomalee

Nicobar Islands (to India)

MALDIVES

Gulf of Mannar

SRI LANKA

INDIAN OCEAN

MALE' ★

INDIAN OCEAN

Negombo

Kandy

COLOMBO ★

Galle

Maldives

0   200   400 kilometres

0   200   400 miles

0   200 km

0   200 miles

Sri Lanka

Sri Lanka exports more tea than any other country.

To find out more about South Asia go to:
www.pandg-atlas.com

Arabian Sea

1

2

3

4

5

6

7

8

9

10

11

12

K   L   M   N   O   P   Q   R   S   T

East Asia

ASIA

A large part of East Asia has a landscape of high mountains, desert or steppe land. Some areas are remote, with long distances between towns, and the climate is extreme. In the southeast the land changes from mountains to wide river valleys and open plains. To the east is Japan, which has a rugged, mountainous landscape. Japan is one of the richest nations in the world. It does not have many natural resources, so it imports them. Japan is well known for making advanced electronic equipment. It is also a world leader in vehicle manufacturing. China and South Korea now have strong economies.

Country File

China

Japan

Mongolia

North Korea

South Korea

Taiwan

Did you know?

◇ Today more people live in Tokyo, which is the capital of Japan, than any other city in the world.

◇ Only about 15% of the land in Japan is suitable for farming, but Japan grows enough rice to feed its population.

KAZAKHSTAN

ALTAI MOUNTAINS

DZUNGARIAN BASIN

KYRGYZSTAN

TIEN SHAN

Urumqi

TAJIKISTAN

TARIM BASIN

PAKISTAN

(Claimed by India)

K2 8611m

TAKLA MAKAN DESERT

KUNLUN MOUNTAINS

ALTUN SHAN

QILIAN Sh

QAIDAM BASIN

(Administered by China, claimed by India)

(Administered by China, claimed by India)

INDIA

PLATEAU OF TIBET

C

H

Salween

HIMALAYAS

Tibet

NEPAL

Brahmaputra

Lhasa

China

Mt Everest 8850m

BHUTAN

INDIA

BURMA

Mek

LA

Great Wall of China

The Great Wall of China is one of the largest structures in the world and it can be seen from space. It starts near the Chinese coast and stretches inland, across northern China, for over 6,400 kilometres. This huge wall was started in 220 BCE and took 10 years to build. It was made to keep out invaders from the north, such as the Mongols.

Traditional herbal medicine, such as these wolf berries, has been used in China for over 4,500 years.

Did you know?

◇ The official language of China is Mandarin, and more people speak this than any other language in the world.

◇ More than one-fifth of the world's population live in China. Most live in the southeast.

◇ In some areas of Mongolia, the temperature drops to -59°C, which is as cold as the Arctic.

Giant panda

These are among the most endangered animals in the world. There are only about 1,600 left in the wild. Pandas are classed as carnivores (meat eaters), but 99 per cent of their diet is bamboo. Pandas live in thick bamboo forests in central China and spend about 14 hours a day eating!

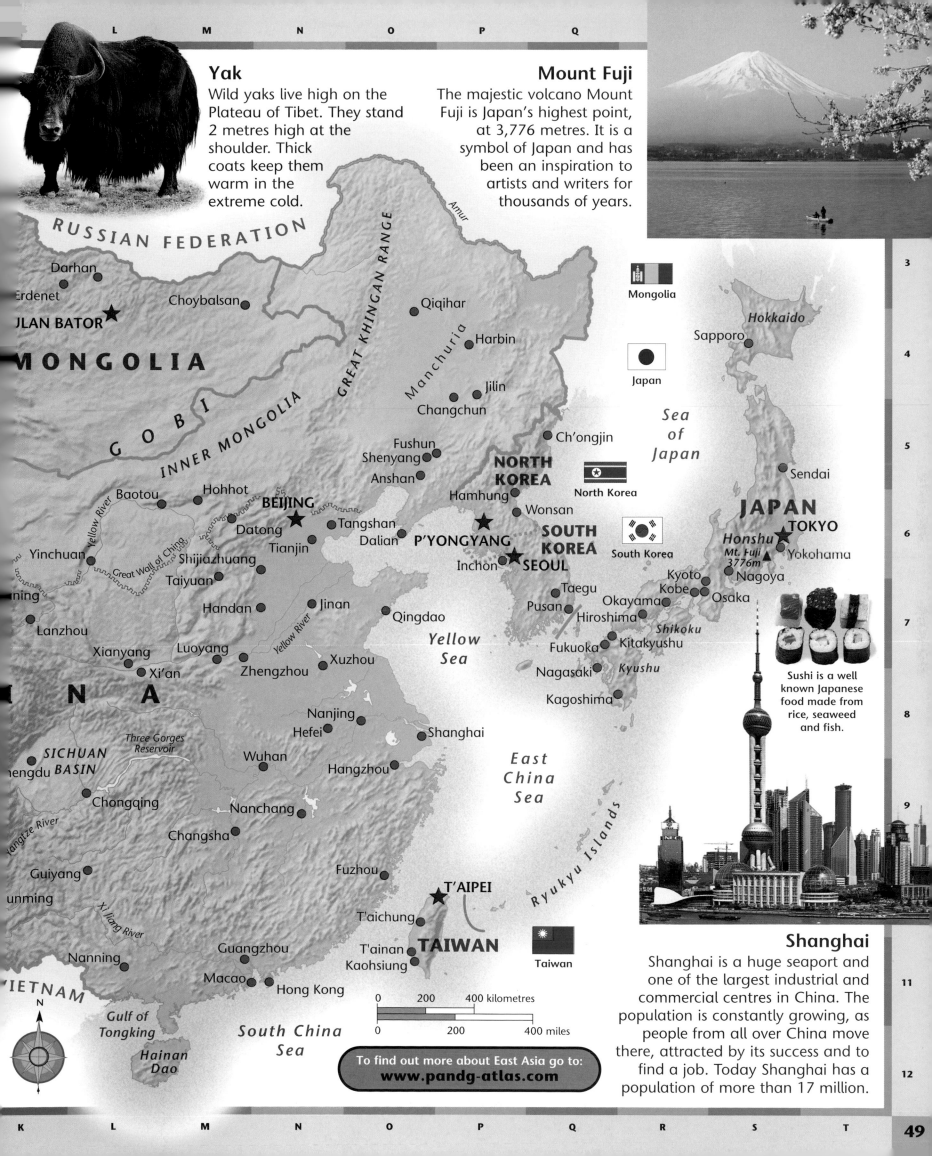

Yak
Wild yaks live high on the Plateau of Tibet. They stand 2 metres high at the shoulder. Thick coats keep them warm in the extreme cold.

Mount Fuji
The majestic volcano Mount Fuji is Japan's highest point, at 3,776 metres. It is a symbol of Japan and has been an inspiration to artists and writers for thousands of years.

Sushi is a well known Japanese food made from rice, seaweed and fish.

Shanghai
Shanghai is a huge seaport and one of the largest industrial and commercial centres in China. The population is constantly growing, as people from all over China move there, attracted by its success and to find a job. Today Shanghai has a population of more than 17 million.

Mongolia

Japan

North Korea

South Korea

Taiwan

RUSSIAN FEDERATION

Darhan
Erdenet
Choybalsan
ULAN BATOR
MONGOLIA
GOBI
INNER MONGOLIA
GREAT KHINGAN RANGE
Amur
Qiqihar
Harbin
Manchuria
Jilin
Changchun
Ch'ongjin
Hokkaido
Sapporo
Sendai

Fushun
Shenyang
Anshan
Hamhung
NORTH KOREA
Wonsan
P'YONGYANG
SOUTH KOREA
SEOUL
Inchon
Sea of Japan
JAPAN
TOKYO
Honshu
Mt. Fuji 3776m
Yokohama
Nagoya

Baotou
Hohhot
BEIJING
Datong
Tianjin
Tangshan
Dalian
Yinchuan
Yellow River
Great Wall of China
Shijiazhuang
Taiyuan
Handan
Jinan
Qingdao
Yellow Sea
Taegu
Pusan
Kyoto
Kobe
Okayama
Osaka
Hiroshima
Shikoku
Fukuoka
Kitakyushu
Nagasaki
Kyushu
Kagoshima

Lanzhou
Xianyang
Luoyang
Xi'an
Zhengzhou
Xuzhou
Yellow River
CHINA
Nanjing
Hefei
Shanghai
SICHUAN BASIN
Three Gorges Reservoir
Chengdu
Wuhan
Hangzhou
East China Sea
Chongqing
Nanchang
Yangtze River
Changsha
Guiyang
Kunming
Fuzhou
Xi Jiang River
T'AIPEI
T'aichung
T'ainan
TAIWAN
Kaohsiung
Guangzhou
Nanning
Macao
Hong Kong
VIETNAM
Gulf of Tongking
Hainan Dao
South China Sea
Ryukyu Islands

0   200   400 kilometres
0   200   400 miles

To find out more about East Asia go to:
www.pandg-atlas.com

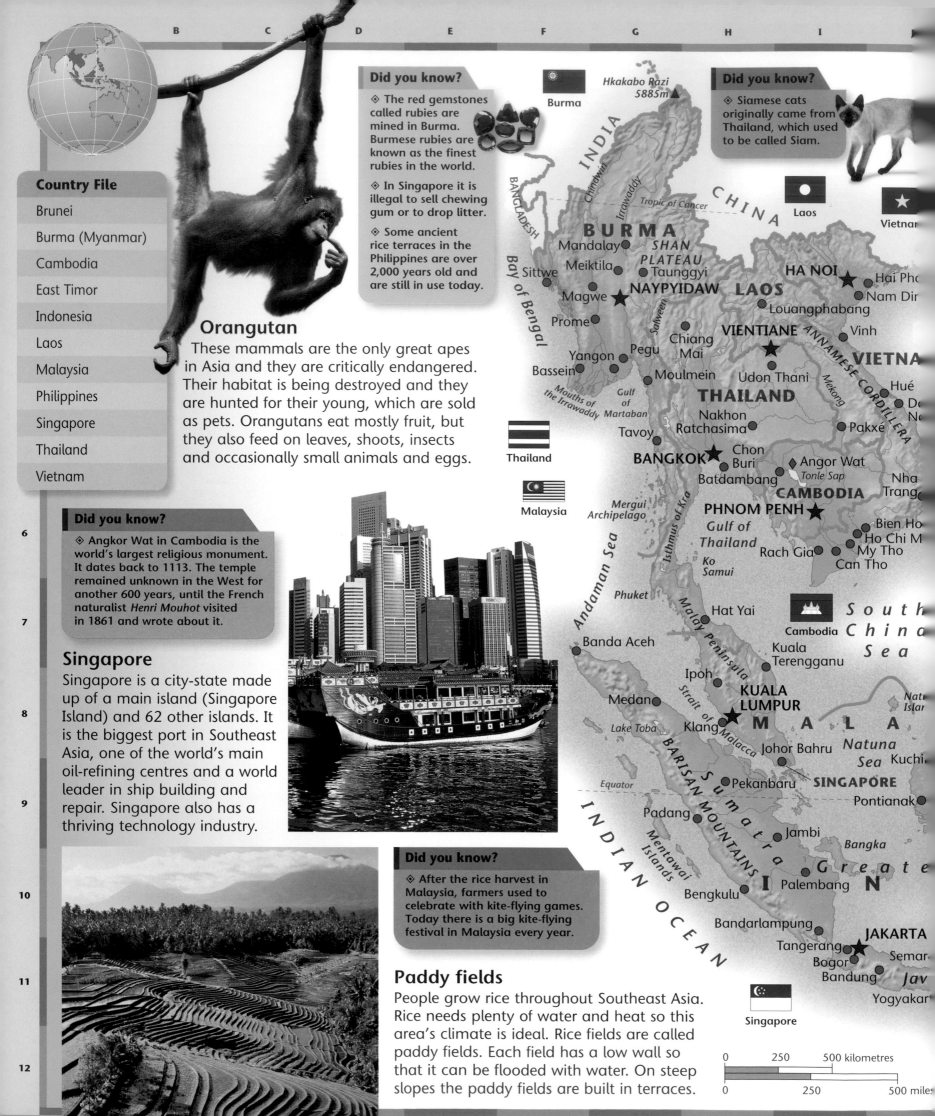

Burma

Hkakabo Razi 5885m

Laos

Vietnam

Country File

- Brunei
- Burma (Myanmar)
- Cambodia
- East Timor
- Indonesia
- Laos
- Malaysia
- Philippines
- Singapore
- Thailand
- Vietnam

Orangutan

These mammals are the only great apes in Asia and they are critically endangered. Their habitat is being destroyed and they are hunted for their young, which are sold as pets. Orangutans eat mostly fruit, but they also feed on leaves, shoots, insects and occasionally small animals and eggs.

Thailand

Malaysia

Singapore

Singapore is a city-state made up of a main island (Singapore Island) and 62 other islands. It is the biggest port in Southeast Asia, one of the world's main oil-refining centres and a world leader in ship building and repair. Singapore also has a thriving technology industry.

Paddy fields

People grow rice throughout Southeast Asia. Rice needs plenty of water and heat so this area's climate is ideal. Rice fields are called paddy fields. Each field has a low wall so that it can be flooded with water. On steep slopes the paddy fields are built in terraces.

Singapore

Map labels

INDIA · CHINA · BANGLADESH · *Chindwin* · *Irrawaddy* · Tropic of Cancer

BURMA · Mandalay · SHAN PLATEAU · Meiktila · Taunggyi · **HA NOI** · Hai Pho · Nam Din · Sittwe · **NAYPYIDAW** · Magwe · Louangphabang · **LAOS** · Prome · **VIENTIANE** · Vinh · Chiang Mai · *Salween* · Bay of Bengal · Yangon · Pegu · Moulmein · **VIETNA** · Bassein · Udon Thani · Hué · Mouths of the Irrawaddy · Gulf of Martaban · **THAILAND** · Nakhon Ratchasima · *Mekong* · Pakxé · De · N · Tavoy · ANNAMESE CORDILLERA · Chon Buri · **BANGKOK** · Angor Wat · Nha Trang · Batdambang · *Tonle Sap* · Mergui Archipelago · **CAMBODIA** · *Isthmus of Kra* · **PHNOM PENH** · Gulf of Thailand · Bien Ho · Ho Chi M · Rach Gia · My Tho · Ko Samui · Can Tho · Andaman Sea · Phuket · Hat Yai · **South China Sea** · Banda Aceh · Kuala Terengganu · Ipoh · *Malay Peninsula* · Medan · **KUALA LUMPUR** · Lake Toba · Klang · *Strait of Malacca* · **MALA** · Johor Bahru · Natuna Sea · Kuchi · Equator · Pekanbaru · **SINGAPORE** · Pontianak · Padang · *Sumatra* · BARISAN MOUNTAINS · Jambi · Bangka · Mentawai Islands · *Greate* · Bengkulu · Palembang · Bandarlampung · **JAKARTA** · INDIAN OCEAN · Tangerang · Semar · Bogor · Bandung · Jav · Yogyakar

```
0      250      500 kilometres
0      250      500 miles
```

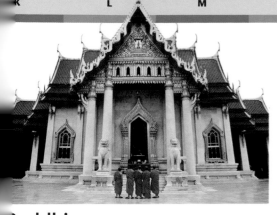

Southeast Asia

ASIA

Much of Southeast Asia is mountainous and covered in thick forest. This area has a tropical monsoon climate, when half of the year is wet and half is dry. Most of the people live in the river valleys, on the fertile plains of the mainland or around the coasts of the islands. Some islands have no people living on them, but others, such as Java, have a big population. People in this area are from many different cultures. They follow lots of religions and speak hundreds of languages. The main industries are processing raw materials, such as oil, minerals, timber and food. Recently, the manufacturing of electronic goods and also computers has increased.

Buddhism

One of the main religions in this area is Buddhism. Buddhist temples have steep roofs, pointed windows and carved details. Like many Buddhist temples, this one is guarded by statues of lions at the entrance.

N

Luzon

Baguio

Philippine Sea

Philippines

★ MANILA

Mindoro

Samar

PHILIPPINES

Panay

Bacolod   Cebu

Negros

Palawan

Sulu
Sea

Cagayan de Oro

Mindanao

Zamboanga

Davao

Lemongrass, lime and coriander are important ingredients in Southeast Asian cooking.

Did you know?

◇ The sultan of Brunei has the largest palace in the world, built of marble, gold mosaics and stained glass.

Brunei

BANDAR
SERI
BEGAWAN
Kota
Kinabalu
★
BRUNEI

Mount Kinabalu
▲ 4101m

Sandakan

Sulu Archipelago

I
A

Celebes
Sea

PACIFIC
OCEAN

Komodo dragon

This is the largest lizard and it grows to 3 metres long. Komodo dragons live on the Lesser Sunda Islands. Their teeth are serrated and their mouths are full of deadly bacteria. They are fierce predators and eat anything that they can overpower.

Borneo

Samarinda

Makassar Strait

Palu

Manado

Halmahera

Equator

Molucca
Sea

East Timor

Jayapura

Papua

Balikpapan

Sulawesi

Buru

Ceram

I

Puncak Jaya ▲ A
4884m

CENTRAL
RANGE

PAPUA
NEW GUINEA

unda Islands

Banjarmasin

N

E

S

Kendari

Ambon

Makassar

Banda
Sea

Aru
Islands

Unusual carved wooden masks like this one are worn by professional dancers in Indonesia.

ava Sea

Flores
Sea

Lesser Sunda Islands

Surabaya

Malang   Bali

Denpasar

Lombok

Mataram

Sumbawa

Flores

★ DILI

EAST
TIMOR

Timor
Sea

Arafura
Sea

Did you know?

◇ Indonesia is made up of more than 17,500 islands. A group of islands like this is called an archipelago. This is one of the most volcanic parts of the world.

Sumba

Kupang

Timor

To find out more about Southeast Asia go to:
www.pandg-atlas.com

Indonesia

Australia

AUSTRALASIA AND OCEANIA

Country File

Australia

This massive country is mostly made up of desert, which is so hot and dry that it is not suitable for farming or for people to live there. The wildest, driest and emptiest parts of the Australian desert are sometimes called 'the outback'. Most of the 20 million people in Australia live in towns along the coast, such as Brisbane, Melbourne and Sydney in the east and Perth in the southwest. The first inhabitants of this continent were the Aboriginal Australians. Today, most Australians are descended from European people who migrated there from the 18th century onwards. Australia has one of the world's biggest mining industries. Copper, gold, coal and opals are all mined there. Other important Australian industries include tourism and wine making. High-quality Australian wines are exported worldwide.

97 per cent of all opals are found in Australia.

INDIAN OCEAN

KIMBERLEY PLATEAU

Broome

Port Hedland

Dampier

GREAT SANDY DESERT

HAMERSLEY RANGE

Lake Mackay

GIBSON DESERT

Tropic of Capricorn

A U

WESTERN AUSTRALIA

GREAT VICTOR DESERT

Geraldton

Kalgoorlie

NULLARBOR

Perth ★

Fremantle

Mandurah

Bunbury

Cape Leeuwin

Albany

Great A

SOUTHER

| 0 | 200 | 400 kilometres |
| 0 | 200 | 400 miles |

Uluru

The magnificent rock called Uluru is the top of an enormous sandstone hill that is buried beneath the desert in Northern Territory. It is also known as Ayers Rock. This is the world's biggest single rock. Uluru rises nearly 350 metres above the surrounding land and it is 9.4 kilometres around the base. This ancient rock is a sacred place for many Aboriginal Australians.

Kangaroo

Kangaroos are mammals called marsupials. The females carry their young in a pouch. Other marsupials in Australia are wallabies, possums and the koala. The only egg-laying mammals – the platypus and echidna – also live in Australia. They are called monotremes.

To find out more about Australia go to:
www.pandg-atlas.com

Arafura Sea

Cape York

Darwin

Did you know?
◈ Australia is the only country that is also a continent on its own. It is the smallest and also the flattest continent in the world.

N

ARNHEM LAND

Gulf of Carpentaria

BARKLY TABLELAND

CAPE YORK PENINSULA

Coral Sea

NAMI ESERT

NORTHERN TERRITORY

GREAT BARRIER REEF

Cairns

Great Barrier Reef
The Great Barrier Reef is made up of over 2,800 coral reefs and is home to more than 1,500 species of fish. It covers an enormous area – 350,000 square kilometres – and is so large that it can be seen from space.

Townsville

Australia

MACDONNELL RANGES

Alice Springs

QUEENSLAND

Mackay

T R A L I A

Rockhampton

Gladstone

Uluru (Ayers Rock) 867m

SIMPSON DESERT

Hervey Bay

Maroochydore-Mooloolaba
Sunshine Coast

Koala
The koala is a marsupial mammal that lives in eucalyptus trees and eats the leaves. Many of these trees are being cut down to make more space for roads and buildings. Koalas are now endangered animals.

SOUTH AUSTRALIA

Lake Eyre North

Coober Pedy

Toowoomba

Brisbane

Gold Coast

Lake Torrens

Lake Frome

FLINDERS RANGES

Lake Gairdner

Darling River

NEW SOUTH WALES

Broken Hill

Coffs Harbour

Port Macquarie

GREAT DIVIDING RANGE

ian Bight

Mildura

Bathurst

Newcastle

CEAN

Adelaide

Murray River

Wagga Wagga

Sydney

Nowra   Wollongong

Kangaroo Island

Albury

Mount Kosciuszko 2228m

CANBERRA

AUSTRALIAN CAPITAL TERRITORY

PACIFIC OCEAN

Bendigo

VICTORIA

AUSTRALIAN ALPS

Ballarat

Geelong   Melbourne

Did you know?
◈ About 140 species of land snake and 32 species of sea snake are found in Australia.

◈ The inland taipan has the strongest venom of any land snake. The venom in one bite could kill 100 people.

Bass Strait

Launceston

TASMANIA

Hobart

Sydney Opera House
Sydney is the biggest and oldest city in Australia, and the Sydney Opera House is one of the most famous buildings in the world. Over 100 million people have visited it.

53

Pacific Islands
AUSTRALASIA AND OCEANIA

There are thousands of islands in the Pacific Ocean, and people from many cultures live there, speaking many languages. The islands are traditionally divided into these groups: Melanesia, Micronesia and Polynesia. The earliest people in this region settled on the island of New Guinea over 40,000 years ago. In the 19th century, the islands were colonized by Europeans, who brought their own cultures, languages and religions. Most of the islands are now part of independent countries. They rely on agriculture and fishing for their income, and some tourism. The islands also export copra, which comes from coconuts. It is made into coconut oil, which is used in soap and cosmetics.

Country File

- Fiji
- Kiribati
- Marshall Islands
- Micronesia
- Nauru
- Palau
- Papua New Guinea
- Samoa
- Solomon Islands
- Tonga
- Tuvalu
- Vanuatu

Onions, limes, ginger, garlic and lemon juice are all traditional ingredients of many south Pacific island dishes.

Did you know?
◇ Nauru is the world's smallest republic and it has an area of only 21 sq km.

◇ Throughout the Pacific islands, pit-roasted foods, including pigs, are eaten on special occasions and for religious celebrations.

Tropic of Cancer

NORTHERN MARIANA ISLANDS (to US)

Marshall

Micronesia

GUAM (to US)
HAGATNA

M

Palau

OREOR
PALAU

Yap
Babeldaob

MICRONESIA

Chuuk Islands

PALIH
Pohnpei

Caroline Islan

Papua New Guinea

Equator

INDONESIA

PAPUA NEW GUINEA

Mount Wilhelm 4509m

New Britain

PORT MORESBY

Guadalcan
HONIA

Coral Sea

AUSTRALIA

CALE

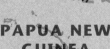
Solomon Islands

Tropic of Co

Vanuatu

Fishing

The people of the Pacific islands fish mainly to feed themselves, but many fish are also caught in the northern Pacific by big fishing boats from Japan, South Korea, Taiwan and the USA. Tuna is a prized fish and the finest tuna can sell for thousands of dollars per fish, especially in Japan. Today much of the commercial fishing of tuna is done using long fishing lines instead of nets.

Doria's tree kangaroo

Nine of the 11 species of tree kangaroo live in the rainforest on the island of New Guinea. The other two live in Australia. Doria's tree kangaroo is the largest one, weighing up to 13 kilograms. Like all kangaroos, it is a marsupial.

Did you know?
◇The Pacific Ocean has lots of volcanic activity. Most of the Pacific islands were formed by volcanoes under the sea.

Papua New Guinea

New Guinea is the second largest island in the world, and Papua New Guinea takes up the eastern half, as well as several smaller islands. About 80 per cent of the population live in groups in the countryside. People live as they have done for many hundreds of years, with traditional ways of life, customs and beliefs.

Did you know?
◇ Papua New Guinea has more ethnic variety than any other country, and it has more than 820 living languages.

◇ Sugarcane probably first came from New Guinea, the island partly occupied by Papua New Guinea.

◇ The coconut tree is called 'the tree of life' by many islanders because every part of it is used or eaten.

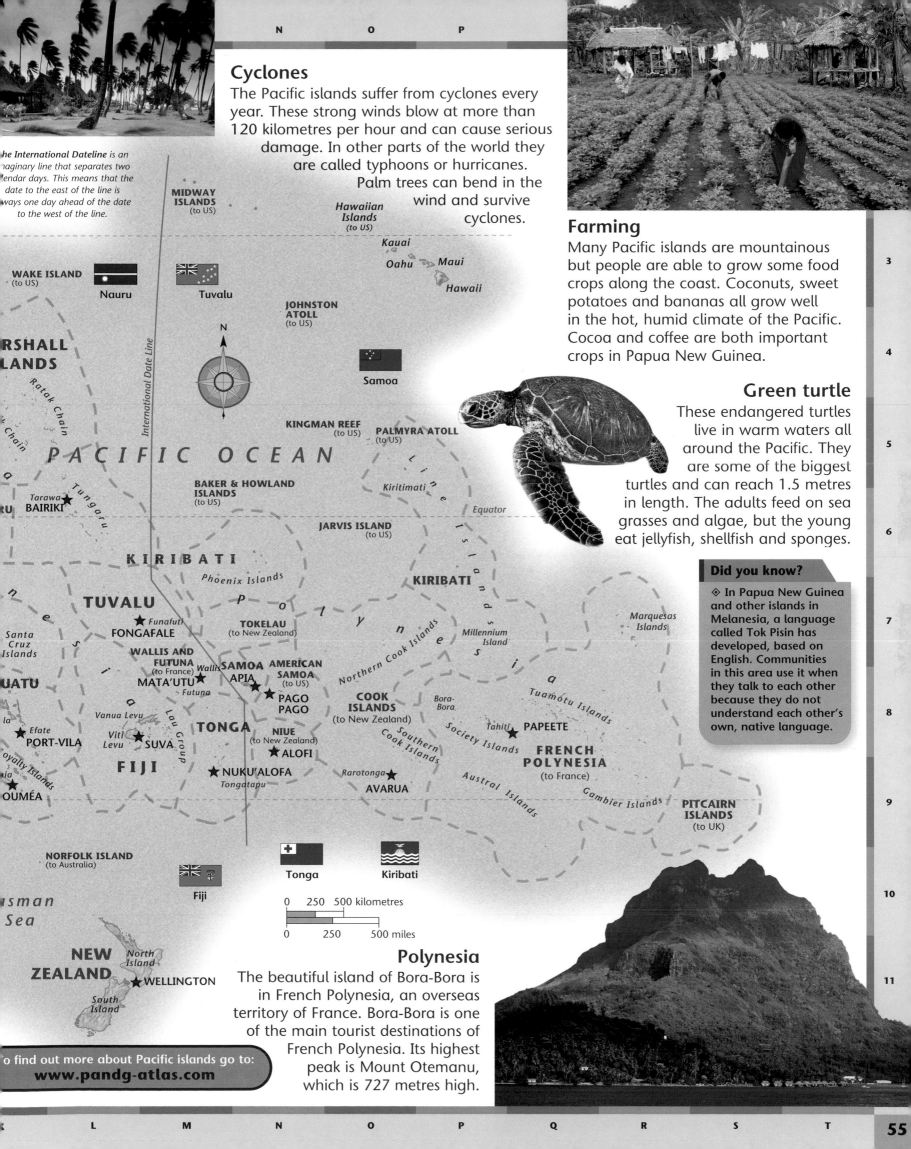

Cyclones

The Pacific islands suffer from cyclones every year. These strong winds blow at more than 120 kilometres per hour and can cause serious damage. In other parts of the world they are called typhoons or hurricanes. Palm trees can bend in the wind and survive cyclones.

Farming

Many Pacific islands are mountainous but people are able to grow some food crops along the coast. Coconuts, sweet potatoes and bananas all grow well in the hot, humid climate of the Pacific. Cocoa and coffee are both important crops in Papua New Guinea.

Green turtle

These endangered turtles live in warm waters all around the Pacific. They are some of the biggest turtles and can reach 1.5 metres in length. The adults feed on sea grasses and algae, but the young eat jellyfish, shellfish and sponges.

Did you know?

◈ In Papua New Guinea and other islands in Melanesia, a language called Tok Pisin has developed, based on English. Communities in this area use it when they talk to each other because they do not understand each other's own, native language.

he International Dateline is an maginary line that separates two endar days. This means that the date to the east of the line is ways one day ahead of the date to the west of the line.

MIDWAY ISLANDS (to US)

Hawaiian Islands (to US)

Kauai
Oahu   Maui
Hawaii

WAKE ISLAND (to US)

Nauru

Tuvalu

JOHNSTON ATOLL (to US)

N

Samoa

RSHALL LANDS

Ratak Chain

Chain

International Date Line

P A C I F I C   O C E A N

KINGMAN REEF (to US)

PALMYRA ATOLL (to US)

Line Islands

Tarawa
BAIRIKI

Tungaru

Kiritimati

BAKER & HOWLAND ISLANDS (to US)

Equator

JARVIS ISLAND (to US)

K I R I B A T I

Phoenix Islands

KIRIBATI

Marquesas Islands

TUVALU

Santa Cruz Islands

Funafuti
FONGAFALE

TOKELAU (to New Zealand)

Millennium Island

P o l y n e s i a

WALLIS AND FUTUNA (to France)
Wallis

SAMOA
APIA

AMERICAN SAMOA (to US)

MATA'UTU

Futuna

PAGO PAGO

Northern Cook Islands

COOK ISLANDS (to New Zealand)

Bora-Bora

Tuamotu Islands

UATU

Vanua Levu

Society Islands

Tahiti **PAPEETE**

Efate
PORT-VILA

Viti Levu

SUVA

TONGA

NIUE (to New Zealand)

Southern Cook Islands

FRENCH POLYNESIA (to France)

la

Lau Group

ALOFI

yalty Islands
ia

FIJI

NUKU'ALOFA
Tongatapu

Rarotonga

Austral Islands

Gambier Islands

PITCAIRN ISLANDS (to UK)

OUMÉA

AVARUA

NORFOLK ISLAND (to Australia)

Tonga

Kiribati

Fiji

0   250   500 kilometres

0   250   500 miles

sman Sea

NEW ZEALAND

North Island

WELLINGTON

South Island

Polynesia

The beautiful island of Bora-Bora is in French Polynesia, an overseas territory of France. Bora-Bora is one of the main tourist destinations of French Polynesia. Its highest peak is Mount Otemanu, which is 727 metres high.

o find out more about Pacific islands go to:
www.pandg-atlas.com

3
4
5
6
7
8
9
10
11

New Zealand

AUSTRALASIA AND OCEANIA

This country in the south Pacific Ocean is similar in size to the United Kingdom. It consists of two main islands – North Island and South Island – and several smaller islands. New Zealand is well known for its spectacular scenery. The landscape includes mountains, volcanoes, long sandy beaches, deep fjords and lush rainforests. It has cool, wet winters and warm, wet summers. New Zealand is one of the world's least populated countries, with 4.25 million people. The first people to settle there about 1,000 years ago were the Polynesians. They became known as the Maoris. For the past 160 years people have migrated there from many countries. Tourism, fishing and hi-tech manufacturing are important industries.

Country File

New Zealand

Auckland

The largest city in New Zealand is Auckland, and about one-third of the population lives there. More than 60 per cent of residents are descended from Europeans and 11 per cent are Maori. This city is very popular with immigrants. Nobody in Auckland lives more than half an hour away from a beach, and the weather is warm all year round.

Did you know?

◇ New Zealand was one of the last places on Earth to be inhabited by people.

◇ Almost one-third of New Zealand is covered by forest. Many of the forests contain unusual species of trees that are found only on these islands, such as kauri trees, which are some of the oldest trees on Earth.

◇ Wine making is a fast-growing industry in New Zealand, and the wines are exported worldwide.

This wooden Maori Tiki carving represents the first man. Tiki carvings are thought of as powerful good luck symbols.

Whale watching

One of the best places to see whales and dolphins in the wild is near the town of Kaikoura, on the east coast of South Island. New Zealand's whales, dolphins and seals are protected, and visitors from all over the world travel to Kaikoura to see them. The whale is a spiritual symbol for the Maoris.

Aoraki/Mount Cook

The highest mountain in New Zealand is Aoraki/Mount Cook in the Southern Alps. It is 3,754 metres high. In Maori legend, these mountains are Aoraki and his three brothers, who are the sons of the Sky Father. They were stranded in their canoe and were frozen by the cold south wind. Their canoe became South Island.

Did you know?

◈ The New Zealand rugby union team is known as the 'All Blacks'. All the players perform the *haka*, a traditional Maori dance, before every game.

◈ Aoraki/Mount Cook used to be about 10m taller than it is now. In 1991, a huge amount of rock and ice fell off the summit in a landslide.

Apples and pears have been grown in the region around Nelson since the 1850s. Most of the fruit is exported to Europe.

0   100   200 kilometres

0   100   200 miles

Kiwi

The kiwi is the national symbol of New Zealand. This bird is about the size of a chicken. It cannot fly, so it is at risk from predators, especially domestic cats and dogs. There are only about 70,000 of these birds left in the wild.

Geysers and springs

The area around Rotorua on North Island is famous for its geysers, hot springs and boiling mud, which are all heated deep inside the Earth. Geysers have a spiritual meaning for the Maoris and almost all have names. The largest is Pohutu, which shoots up to 30 metres into the air.

North Cape

Whangarei

Great Barrier Island

Auckland

Manurewa

Bay of Plenty

East Cape

Hamilton

Tauranga

Lake Rotorua

Whakatane

Rotorua

Lake Taupo

Taupo

Gisborne

New Plymouth

Cape Egmont

North Island

Mount Ruapehu 2797m

Mount Taranaki 2518m

Napier

Wanganui

Hastings

Rangitikei

NEW

ZEALAND

Masterton

Cook Strait

Lower Hutt

WELLINGTON

Cape Palliser

PACIFIC OCEAN

N

New Zealand

enheim

Wairau

Clarence

Kairkoura

Waimakariri

hristchurch

Banks Peninsula

Milford Sound

One of the most beautiful places in New Zealand is Milford Sound in the fjord lands of South Island. It is over 15 kilometres long and is surrounded by sheer cliffs rising more than 1,200 metres on each side. There are lush rainforests clinging to the sides of the fjord, and seals, dolphins and penguins swim in the waters. One of the world's most popular walks, the Milford Track, finishes here.

Did you know?

◈ About two-thirds of New Zealand's energy comes from hydroelectricity, which is produced by its fast-flowing rivers. The water is used to turn huge wheels called turbines, which in turn power an electric generator.

◈ New Zealand produces about 25% of the world's 'strong wool', which is used to make wool products that need to be hardwearing, such as carpets and rugs.

Hooker's sea lion

These sea lions are found only in New Zealand, mostly around the Auckland Islands. In the breeding season, a male lives with a group of up to 25 females. These sea lions can swim over 125 kilometres to find food, which includes squid, crabs, crayfish and fish.

There are about 40 million sheep in New Zealand. New Zealand lamb is famous all over the world.

To find out more about New Zealand go to:
www.pandg-atlas.com

Arctic Circle

Bering Strait

USA (Alaska)

Chukchi Sea

Wrangel Island

East Siberian Sea

New Siberian Islands

Limit of summer pack ice

Beaufort Sea

Limit of permanent ice cap

R U S S I A N   F E D E R A T I O N

Banks Island

Victoria Island

Melville Island

ARCTIC OCEAN

Laptev Sea

Queen Elizabeth Islands

North Pole

Severnaya Zemlya

Taymyr Peninsula

Ellesmere Island

C A N A D A

Kara Sea

Qaanaaq

Knud Rasmussen Land

Baffin Bay

Wandel Sea

Franz Josef Land

Novaya Zemlya

Baffin Island

Limit of permanent ice cap

SVALBARD (to Norway)

Davis Strait

Limit of summer pack ice

Limit of winter pack ice

Aasiat
Sisimiut

Ilulissat

GREENLAND (to Denmark)

Barents Sea

Maniitsoq

NUUK

Kong Christian IX Land

Greenland Sea

North Cape

Kola Peninsula

Gunnbjørn Fjeld 3,700m

Ittoqqortoormiit

Qaqortoq

Tasiilaq

Norwegian Sea

N O R W A Y

F I N L A N D

Nunap Isua

Denmark Strait

Arctic Circle

REYKJAVIK ★ ICELAND

0   400   800 kilometres

0   400   800 miles

Polar bear

There are 21–25,000 polar bears in the Arctic. These animals are now a threatened species. As the Arctic pack ice continues to melt, polar bears are finding it difficult to hunt for food because they have to swim so far between the bits of ice. Many polar bears are dying as they search for food.

Did you know?

◈ The Arctic Ocean is the smallest ocean in the world. It measures only about 14 million sq km.

◈ By 2030 the Arctic may have ice-free summers because so much ice is melting in summer and not refreezing in winter.

Inuit people once lived by fishing herding and hunting whales, bea and seals. Many still wear clothe made of fur to keep them warm

The Arctic
ASIA, EUROPE AND NORTH AMERICA

The Arctic is a huge area with the North Pole at its centre. It is not a continent or a country but includes the Arctic Ocean and the most northern parts of Asia, North America and Europe. During winter, much of the Arctic Ocean is covered by pack ice about 4 metres thick. During the short summers the ice melts and the area of pack ice shrinks. It grows again when winter returns and temperatures drop to -60°C. Even though the climate is cold, people have lived in the Arctic for thousands of years. The Sami and Inuit people were originally nomads who survived by herding animals and hunting. Today most people live in new towns, but some still live a traditional life.

Northern lights

The *aurora borealis*, or the northern lights, are caused by solar winds reacting with the Earth's upper atmosphere. This colourful effect in the sky can also be seen around the South Pole, where it is known as the southern lights, or *aurora australis*.

Antarctica

ANTARCTICA

This is the fifth largest continent and it is almost twice the size of the USA. Antarctica has a harsh, cold climate and it is the windiest place on Earth. Almost all of Antarctica is covered with a sheet of ice. On average, the ice is 1.6 kilometres thick, and it is thousands of years old. The ice contains most of the fresh water on Earth. Under the ice, the land contains oil and other minerals, including gold, iron ore and coal. Huge blocks of ice often break off the edge of the sheet and float away as icebergs. To protect this wilderness and its wildlife, 46 nations have signed an agreement called the Antarctic Treaty. They agree not to carry out any mining or put a military station there. Antarctica is the only continent where people do not live all year round.

Cold science

Groups of scientists, tourists and explorers are allowed to visit Antarctica. Many things are studied in Antarctica, including how plants and animals can survive there.

Humpbacks and other whales visit the icy seas of Antarctica. When a whale leaps out of the water it is known as 'breaching'.

Did you know?

◇ In winter the temperatures in Antarctica can drop to below -80°C.

◇ Antarctica is unusual because it is not owned by any country.

Emperor penguin

The only penguins that breed in Antarctica during the bitter cold winter are emperor penguins. They weigh over 30 kilograms and are the tallest penguins, at 1.2 metres high. They walk up to 120 kilometres to their breeding grounds.

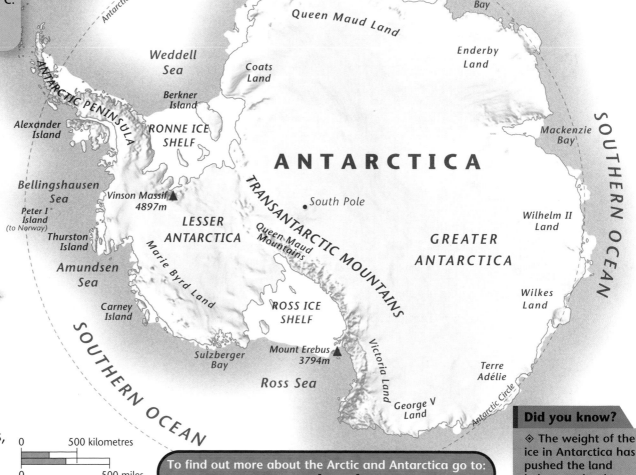

SOUTHERN OCEAN

Antarctic Circle

Queen Maud Land

Lützow-Holm Bay

Weddell Sea

Coats Land

Enderby Land

ANTARCTIC PENINSULA

Berkner Island

RONNE ICE SHELF

Alexander Island

Mackenzie Bay

ANTARCTICA

Bellingshausen Sea

Vinson Massif ▲ 4897m

South Pole

Wilhelm II Land

Peter I Island (to Norway)

Thurston Island

LESSER ANTARCTICA

Queen Maud Mountains

TRANSANTARCTIC MOUNTAINS

GREATER ANTARCTICA

Amundsen Sea

Marie Byrd Land

Carney Island

ROSS ICE SHELF

Wilkes Land

SOUTHERN OCEAN

Sulzberger Bay

Mount Erebus 3794m

Victoria Land

Terre Adélie

Ross Sea

George V Land

Antarctic Circle

SOUTHERN OCEAN

SOUTHERN OCEAN

0   500 kilometres

0   500 miles

To find out more about the Arctic and Antarctica go to:
www.pandg-atlas.com

Did you know?

◇ The weight of the ice in Antarctica has pushed the land below sea level.

3

4

5

6

7

8

9

10

11

12

Index to the maps

In this atlas there is an **Index to the maps** on page 60 and a **General index** on page 68.

Place name index
The **Index to the maps** lists all the names that appear on the maps. Each name is followed by a description, its location, a page number and a grid reference number. Town names do not have a description.

place name   description   location

Anatolia   *physical region* Turkey **10 D5**

page number
grid reference

To find our example 'Anatolia', first go to the page shown—p10, then find the letter 'D' and number '5' around the border of the page. Trace a line down from 'D' and a line across from '5'. The lines meet at the precise square on the grid in which 'Anatolia' can be found.

• • A • •

Aalborg Denmark **33 L10**
Aasiat Greenland **58 B6**
Aberdeen Scotland, UK **35 O2**
Abha Saudi Arabia **43 N10**
Abidjan Ivory Coast **28 H10**
Abu Dhabi *capital city* United Arab Emirates **43 Q8**
Abuja *capital city* Nigeria **28 J10**
Acapulco Mexico **24 G8**
Accra *capital city* Ghana **28 H10**
Aconcagua, Cerro *mountain* Argentina **27 O9**
A Coruña Spain **35 M8**
Adana Turkey **43 L3**
Ad Dahna *desert* Saudi Arabia **43 O7**
Ad Damman Saudi Arabia **43 P7**
Addis Ababa *capital city* Ethiopia **29 O9**
Adelaide *state capital* South Australia **53 M9**
Aden Yemen **43 N12**
Aden, Gulf of *sea feature* NW Indian Ocean **10 E7**
Adriatic Sea *sea* Mediterranean Sea **37 O8**
Aegean Sea *sea* Mediterranean Sea **39 O10**
Afghanistan *country* C Asia **45 M10**
Africa *continent* **10 C7**
Agadez Niger **28 J8**
Agra India **47 N4**
Ahaggar *plateau* Algeria **28 I7**
Ahmadabad India **47 M6**
Ahvaz Iran **43 O5**
Ajaccio France **35 R9**
Akureyri Iceland **33 L1**
Alabama *state* USA **23 P8**
Alai Range *mountain range* Kyrgyzstan/Tajikistan **45 O8**
Alakol, Lake *lake* Kazakhstan **45 R5**
Aland Islands *island group* Finland **33 O8**

Alaska *state* USA **22 G9**
Alaska, Gulf of *sea feature* N Pacific Ocean **22 G10**
Alaska Range *mountain range* USA **11 M3**
Albacete Spain **35 O11**
Albania *country* SE Europe **39 M9**
Albany Western Australia **52 G10**
Albany *state capital* New York, USA **23 R5**
Alberta *province* Canada **20 H7**
Albuquerque New Mexico, USA **23 K8**
Albury New South Wales, Australia **53 O10**
Aldan *river* Russia **41 O8**
Aleppo Syria **43 L4**
Aleutian Islands *island group* USA **11 L4**
Alexander Island *island* Antarctica **59 N8**
Alexandria Egypt **29 M5**
Algeria *country* N Africa **28 I6**
Algiers *capital city* Algeria **28 I4**
Al Hufuf Saudi Arabia **43 P7**
Alicante Spain **35 O11**
Alice Springs Northern Territory, Australia **53 L6**
Al Kut Iraq **43 O5**
Allahabad India **47 O5**
Almaty Kazakhstan **45 Q6**
Al Mukalla Yemen **43 P11**
Alofi *capital city* Niue **55 N8**
Alps *mountain range* C Europe **10 C4**
Altai Mountains *mountain range* C Asia **10 G4**
Altamira Brazil **27 Q4**
Altun Shan *mountain range* China **48 H6**
Amazon *river* C South America **27 Q4**
Amazon Basin *basin* C South America **27 O4**
Ambon Indonesia **51 O10**
American Samoa *US territory* C Pacific Ocean **55 N7**
Amiens France **35 P5**
Amman *capital city* Jordan **43 L5**
Amritsar India **47 M3**
Amsterdam *capital city* Netherlands **35 Q4**
Amu Darya *river* C Asia **45 M9**
Amundsen Sea *sea* Southern Ocean **59 N10**
Amur *river* China/Russia **10 I4**
Anápolis Brazil **27 Q6**
Anatolia *physical region* Turkey **10 D5**
Anchorage Alaska, USA **22 G10**
Andaman Islands *island group* India **47 S9**
Andaman Sea *sea* NE Indian Ocean **50 F7**
Andes *mountain range* W South America **27 M5**
Andijon Uzbekistan **45 P8**
Andorra *country* SW Europe **35 O9**
Andros Island *island* Bahamas **25 M6**
Angara *river* Russia **41 K9**
Angel Falls *waterfall* Venezuela **27 P3**
Angkor Wat *archaeological site* Cambodia **50 I5**
Angola *country* S Africa **30 I7**
Anguilla *UK territory* Caribbean **25 R7**
Ankara *capital city* Turkey **43 K2**
An Nafud *desert* Saudi Arabia **43 M6**
An Najaf Iraq **43 N5**
Annamese Cordillera *mountain range* SE Asia **50 I4**
Annapolis *state capital* Maryland, USA **23 R6**
An Nasiriyah Iraq **43 O6**
Anshan China **49 O5**
Antalya Turkey **43 K3**
Antananarivo *capital city* Madagascar **31 O8**
Antarctica *continent* **59 P8**
Antarctic Peninsula *peninsula* Antarctica **59 N8**
Anticosti Island *island* Canada **21 Q8**
Antigua & Barbuda *country* Caribbean **25 R7**
Antofagasta Chile **27 N7**
Antwerp Belgium **35 Q5**
Aoraki *mountain* New Zealand **56 I9**
Apennines *mountain range* Italy **37 M7**

Apia *capital city* Samoa **55 N8**
Appalachian Mountains *mountain range* USA **23 P7**
Arabian Peninsula *peninsula* SW Asia **43 M7**
Arabian Sea *sea* NW Indian Ocean **10 F6**
Aracaju Brazil **27 S5**
Arafura Sea *sea* SW Pacific Ocean **10 I8**
Araguaia *river* Brazil **27 Q5**
Arak Iran **43 P4**
Aral Sea *lake* Kazakhstan/Uzbekistan **45 L6**
Ararat, Mt *mountain* Turkey **43 N2**
Aras *river* SW Asia **43 O3**
Archangel Russia **40 G6**
Arctic Ocean *ocean* **58 C3**
Arequipa Peru **27 N6**
Argentina *country* S South America **27 O9**
Arhus Denmark **33 L10**
Arica Chile **27 N6**
Arizona *state* USA **22 I8**
Arkansas *state* USA **23 N7**
Arkansas *river* USA **23 N8**
Armenia *country* SW Asia **43 N2**
Arnhem Land *physical region* Australia **53 L2**
Ar Rub' Al Khali *desert* Saudi Arabia **43 O9**
Arta Greece **39 N10**
Aruba *Dutch territory* Caribbean **25 P9**
Aru Islands *island group* Indonesia **51 Q11**
Ascension Island *UK territory* C Atlantic Ocean **12 A8**
Ascension Island *island* C Atlantic Ocean **10 B8**
Asgabat *capital city* Turkmenistan **45 K9**
Ashburton New Zealand **56 J9**
Asia *continent* **10 H4**
Asmara *capital city* Eritrea **29 O8**
As Sib Oman **43 R8**
Astana *capital city* Kazakhstan **45 O3**
Astrakhan' Russia **40 E9**
Asunción *capital city* Paraguay **27 P7**
Aswan Egypt **29 N7**
Atacama Desert *desert* Chile **27 O7**
Athabasca *river* Canada **20 H8**
Athabasca, Lake *lake* Canada **20 I7**
Athens *capital city* Greece **39 O10**
Atlanta *state capital* Georgia, USA **23 P8**
Atlantic Ocean *ocean* **10 B9**
Atlas Mountains *mountain range* NW Africa **28 H5**
At Taif Saudi Arabia **43 M9**
Atyrau Kazakhstan **44 J5**
Auckland New Zealand **57 L3**
Augusta *state capital* Maine, USA **23 S4**
Aurangabad India **47 M7**
Austin *state capital* Texas, USA **23 M9**
Austral Islands *island group* French Polynesia **55 P9**
Australia *country* **52 J6**
Australia *continent* **10 I9**
Australian Alps *mountain range* Australia **53 O10**
Australian Capital Territory *territory* Australia **53 P10**
Austria *country* C Europe **37 O5**
Avarua *capital city* Cook Islands **55 O9**
Ayers Rock *see* Uluru
Azerbaijan *country* SW Asia **43 O2**
Azores *island group* Portugal **34 I11**
Azov, Sea of *sea* Black Sea **39 S6**

• • B • •

Babeldaob *island* Palau **54 H5**
Bab el Mandeb *sea feature* NW Indian Ocean **43 N12**
Babruysk Belarus **39 P2**
Bacau Romania **39 P6**
Bacolod Philippines **51 N6**
Baffin Bay *sea feature* NW Atlantic Ocean **58 B5**
Baffin Island *island* Canada **21 M4**
Baghdad *capital city* Iraq **43 N5**
Baghlan Afghanistan **45 O10**

Baguio Philippines **51 M4**
Bahamas *country* Caribbean **25 N6**
Bahamas *island group* Caribbean **11 Q6**
Bahía Blanca Argentina **27 P10**
Bahrain *country* SW Asia **43 P7**
Baikal, Lake *lake* Russia **41 L10**
Bairiki *capital city* Kiribati **55 L6**
Baja California *peninsula* Mexico **24 D3**
Baker & Howland Islands *US territory* C Pacific Ocean **55 M6**
Baku *capital city* Azerbaijan **43 P2**
Balearic Islands *island group* Spain **35 P11**
Bali *island* Indonesia **51 L11**
Balikpapan Indonesia **51 L9**
Balkanabat Turkmenistan **44 J8**
Balkan Mountains *mountain range* Bulgaria **39 O8**
Balkh Afghanistan **45 N9**
Balkhash, Lake *lake* Kazakhstan **45 P5**
Ballarat Victoria, Australia **53 N10**
Balsas *river* Mexico **24 G7**
Baltic Sea *sea* NE Atlantic Ocean **33 O11**
Baltimore Maryland, USA **23 R6**
Bamako *capital city* Mali **28 G9**
Bamian Afghanistan **45 N10**
Banda Aceh Indonesia **50 F7**
Bandar Seri Begawan *capital city* Brunei **51 L8**
Bandar-e' Abbas Iran **43 R7**
Bandar-e Bushehr Iran **43 P6**
Bandarlampung Indonesia **50 I10**
Banda Sea *sea* W Pacific Ocean **51 O10**
Bandung Indonesia **50 J11**
Bangalore India **47 N9**
Bangka *island* Indonesia **50 I9**
Bangkok *capital city* Thailand **50 H5**
Bangladesh *country* S Asia **47 R5**
Bangui *capital city* Central African Republic **29 L10**
Banja Luka Bosnia & Herzegovina **39 L7**
Banjarmasin Indonesia **51 L10**
Banjul *capital city* Gambia **28 F9**
Banks Island *island* Canada **20 I3**
Banks Peninsula *peninsula* New Zealand **57 K9**
Banska Bystrica Slovakia **37 Q5**
Baotou China **49 M6**
Barbados *country* Caribbean **25 S8**
Barcelona Spain **35 P9**
Barcelona Venezuela **27 O2**
Barents Sea *sea* Arctic Ocean **58 E6**
Bari Italy **37 P9**
Barinas Venezuela **27 N2**
Barisan Mountains *mountain range* Indonesia **50 G8**
Barkley Tableland *plateau* Australia **53 L3**
Barnaul Russia **40 J10**
Barquisimeto Venezuela **27 N2**
Barranquilla Colombia **27 N2**
Basel Switzerland **37 L5**
Basra Iraq **43 O6**
Bassein Burma **50 F4**
Bass Strait *sea feature* Australia **53 O11**
Batdambang Cambodia **50 I5**
Bathurst New South Wales, Australia **53 P9**
Baton Rouge *state capital* Louisiana, USA **23 N9**
Beaufort Sea *sea* Arctic Ocean **58 B2**
Beijing *capital city* China **49 N6**
Beira Mozambique **31 M9**
Beirut *capital city* Lebanon **43 L4**
Belarus *country* E Europe **39 P2**
Belém Brazil **27 R4**
Belfast *province capital* Northern Ireland, UK **35 N3**
Belgium *country* NW Europe **35 Q5**
Belgrade *capital city* Serbia **39 M7**
Belize *country* Central America **25 K8**
Belize City Belize **25 K8**
Bellingshausen Sea *sea* Southern Ocean **59 N9**
Belmopan *capital city* Belize **25 K8**
Belo Horizonte Brazil **27 R7**

NIZHNIY NOVGOROD—RWANDA

Nizhniy Novgorod Russia **40 F7**
Norfolk Island *Australian territory* SW Pacific Ocean **55 L10**
Norilsk Russia **41 K6**
Norrkoping Sweden **33 N9**
North America *continent* **11 O4**
North Cape *headland* New Zealand **57 K1**
North Cape *headland* Norway **33 P1**
North Carolina *state* USA **23 R7**
North Dakota *state* USA **23 L4**
Northern Cook Islands *island group* Cook Islands **55 O8**
Northern Dvina *river* Russia **40 G6**
Northern Ireland *province* UK **35 M3**
Northern Mariana Islands *US territory* W Pacific Ocean **54 I3**
Northern Territory *territory* Australia **53 K4**
North European Plain *plain* N Europe **10 D4**
North Island *island* New Zealand **57 M5**
North Korea *country* E Asia **49 P5**
North Pole *pole* Arctic Ocean **58 D4**
North Sea *sea* NE Atlantic Ocean **10 C4**
North Siberian Lowland *lowland* Russia **41 K6**
Northwest Territories *territory* Canada **20 H5**
Norway *country* N Europe **33 M7**
Norwegian Sea *sea* NE Atlantic Ocean **58 D7**
Nouakchott *capital city* Mauritania **28 F8**
Nouméa *capital city* New Caledonia **55 K9**
Nova Scotia *province* Canada **21 Q10**
Nova Scotia *peninsula* Canada **11 R5**
Novaya Zemlya *island group* Russia **40 I5**
Novi Sad Serbia **39 M7**
Novokuznetsk Russia **40 J10**
Novosibirsk Russia **40 J9**
Nowra New South Wales, Australia **53 P10**
Nuku'alofa *capital city* Tonga **55 M9**
Nukus Uzbekistan **45 L7**
Nullarbor Plain *plain* Australia **52 I8**
Nunap Isua *headland* Greenland **58 A7**
Nunavut *territory* Canada **21 K5**
Nuuk *capital city* Greenland **58 A6**
Nyasa, Lake *lake* S Africa **31 M7**
Nyiregyhaza Hungary **39 N5**

• • O • •

Oahu *island* Hawaii, USA **22 I11**
Oakland California, USA **22 G6**
Oamaru New Zealand **56 J10**
Oaxaca Mexico **24 H8**
Ob' *river* Russia **40 I7**
Odense Denmark **33 L11**
Oder *river* C Europe **37 O2**
Odesa Ukraine **39 Q6**
Ohio *state* USA **23 P6**
Ohio *river* USA **23 P6**
Ohrid, Lake *lake* Albania/Macedonia **39 M9**
Okavango *river* S Africa **30 J8**
Okavango Delta *wetland* Botswana **30 J9**
Okayama Japan **49 R7**
Okeechobee, Lake *lake* USA **23 R10**
Okhotsk, Sea of *sea* NW Pacific Ocean **41 Q8**
Oklahoma *state* USA **23 M8**
Oklahoma City *state capital* Oklahoma, USA **23 M7**
Oland *island* Sweden **33 O10**
Olduvai Gorge *valley* Tanzania **31 M5**
Olympia *state capital* Washington, USA **22 H3**
Omaha Nebraska, USA **23 M6**
Oman *country* SW Asia **43 R9**
Oman, Gulf of *sea feature* NW Indian Ocean **43 R7**
Omdurman Sudan **29 N8**
Omsk Russia **40 I9**
Onega, Lake *lake* Russia **40 F6**
Ontario *province* Canada **21 L8**
Ontario, Lake *lake* Canada/USA **23 R4**
Oporto Portugal **35 L9**
Oran Algeria **28 I4**
Orange River *river* S Africa **30 J10**
Orebro *town* Sweden **33 N9**
Oregon *state* USA **22 H4**
Orenburg Russia **40 G9**
Oreor *capital city* Palau **54 H5**
Orinoco *river* Colombia/Venezuela **27 O2**
Orkney Islands *island group* Scotland, UK **35 O1**
Orlando Florida, USA **23 Q9**
Orléans France **35 P6**
Orumiyeh Iran **43 N3**
Oruro Bolivia **27 O6**
Osaka Japan **49 R7**
Osh Kyrgyzstan **45 P8**
Oshawa Ontario, Canada **21 N11**
Osijek Croatia **39 M6**
Oslo *capital city* Norway **33 M8**
Ostersund Sweden **33 N6**
Ostrava Czech Republic **37 P4**
Ottawa *capital city* Ontario, Canada **21 O10**
Ouagadougou *capital city* Burkina Faso **28 H9**
Oulu Finland **33 Q5**
Ounasjoki *river* Finland **33 Q4**
Outer Hebrides *island group* Scotland, UK **35 M1**
Oviedo Spain **35 M8**

• • P • •

Pacific Ocean *ocean* **11 L5**
Padang Indonesia **50 H9**
Pago Pago *capital city* American Samoa **55 N8**
Pakistan *country* S Asia **47 K3**
Pakxé Laos **50 I5**
Palau *country* W Pacific Ocean **54 G5**
Palawan *island* Philippines **51 L6**
Palembang Indonesia **50 I10**
Palermo Italy **37 N11**
Palikir *capital city* Micronesia **54 J5**
Palk Strait *sea feature* N Indian Ocean **47 O10**
Palliser, Cape *headland* New Zealand **57 L7**
Palma Spain **35 P10**
Palmyra Atoll *US territory* C Pacific Ocean **55 O5**
Palu Indonesia **51 M9**
Pamir *river* Afghanistan/Tajikistan **45 P9**
Pamirs *mountain range* C Asia **45 P9**
Pampas *plain* Argentina **27 O9**
Panama *country* Central America **25 M11**
Panama Canal *canal* Panama **25 M10**
Panama City *capital city* Panama **25 M10**
Panay *island* Philippines **51 M6**
Papeete *capital city* French Polynesia **55 Q8**
Papua *province* Indonesia **51 R10**
Papua New Guinea *country* SW Pacific Ocean **54 I6**
Paracel Islands *disputed territory* SE Asia **12 H6**
Paraguay *country* C South America **27 P7**
Paraguay *river* C South America **11 R9**
Paramaribo *capital city* Suriname **27 Q2**
Paraná *river* C South America **27 P8**
Paris *capital city* France **35 P6**
Patagonia *physical region* Argentina/Chile **27 O11**
Patna India **47 Q5**
Patos, Lagoa dos *sea feature* SW Atlantic Ocean **27 Q8**
Patra Greece **39 N10**
Pavlodar Kazakhstan **45 P3**
Peace *river* Canada **20 I7**
Pechora *river* Russia **40 H6**
Pecs Hungary **39 M6**
Pegu Burma **50 G4**
Peipus, Lake *lake* Estonia **33 Q9**
Pekanbaru Indonesia **50 H9**
Peloponnese *peninsula* Greece **39 N11**
Pennsylvania *state* USA **23 Q5**
Penza Russia **40 F8**
Perm' Russia **40 G8**
Perpignan France **35 P9**
Perth *state capital* Western Australia **52 G9**
Peru *country* W South America **27 M5**
Peshawar Pakistan **47 L2**
Peter I Island *Norwegian territory* Southern Ocean **59 N9**
Petra *archaeological site* Jordan **43 L6**
Petropavlovsk Kazakhstan **45 O2**
Petropavlovsk-Kamchatskiy Russia **41 R8**
Petrozavodsk Russia **40 F6**
Philadelphia *town* Pennsylvania, USA **23 R5**
Philippine Islands *island group* SE Asia **10 I7**
Philippines *country* SE Asia **51 M6**
Philippine Sea *sea* W Pacific Ocean **10 I6**
Phnom Penh *capital city* Cambodia **50 I6**
Phoenix *state capital* Arizona, USA **22 I8**
Phoenix Islands *island group* Kiribati **55 M7**
Phuket *island* Thailand **50 G7**
Pierre *state capital* South Dakota, USA **23 L5**
Pinar del Rio Cuba **25 L6**
Pindos Mountains *mountain range* Greece **39 N10**
Piraeus Greece **39 O10**
Pitcairn Islands *UK territory* C Pacific Ocean **55 R9**
Pitcairn Islands *island group* S Pacific Ocean **11 N9**
Pittsburgh Pennsylvania, USA **23 Q6**
Piura Peru **27 M4**
Plata, Río de la *sea feature* SW Atlantic Ocean **27 P9**
Plenty, Bay of *sea feature* New Zealand **57 M4**
Ploiesti Romania **39 P7**
Plovdiv Bulgaria **39 O8**
Plymouth England, UK **35 N5**
Plzen Czech Republic **37 N4**
Po *river* Italy **37 M7**
Pobedy, Pik *mountain* China/Kyrgyzstan **45 R7**
Podgorica *capital city* Montenegro **39 M8**
Pohnpei *island* Micronesia **54 J5**
Pokhara Nepal **47 P4**
Poland *country* C Europe **37 P3**
Poltava Ukraine **39 R4**
Polynesia *island group* C Pacific Ocean **55 N7**
Pontianak Indonesia **50 J9**
Port-au-Prince *capital city* Haiti **25 O7**
Port Elizabeth South Africa **31 K11**
Port Hedland Western Australia **52 G5**
Portland Oregon, USA **22 H4**
Port Louis *capital city* Mauritius **31 P9**
Port Macquarie New South Wales, Australia **53 Q8**
Port Moresby *capital city* Papua New Guinea **54 I7**
Porto Alegre Brazil **27 Q8**
Porto-Novo *capital city* Benin **28 I10**
Porto Velho Brazil **27 O5**
Port Sudan Sudan **29 O7**
Portugal *country* SW Europe **35 M10**
Port-Vila *capital city* Vanuatu **55 K8**
Potosí Bolivia **27 O7**
Po Valley *valley* Italy **37 M7**
Poznan Poland **37 P3**
Prague *capital city* Czech Republic **37 O4**
Praia *capital city* Cape Verde **28 E8**
Prespa, Lake *lake* SE Europe **39 N9**
Pretoria *see* Tshwane
Prince Edward Island *province* Canada **21 Q9**
Prince Edward Islands *island group* South Africa **10 D10**
Prince George British Columbia, Canada **20 G8**
Pripet *river* Belarus/Ukraine **39 P3**
Pripet Marshes *wetland* Belarus/Ukraine **39 O3**
Pristina *capital city* Kosovo **39 N8**
Prome Burma **50 G4**
Providence *state capital* Rhode Island, USA **23 S5**
Prudhoe Bay Alaska, USA **22 G9**
Prut *river* SE Europe **39 P6**
Puebla Mexico **24 H7**
Puerto Ayacucho Venezuela **27 O2**
Puerto Montt Chile **27 N10**
Puerto Rico *US territory* Caribbean **25 Q7**
Puncak Jaya *mountain* Indonesia **51 R10**
Pune India **47 M7**
Punta Arenas Chile **27 O12**
Purus *river* Brazil/Peru **27 O4**
Pusan South Korea **49 Q7**
Putumayo *river* N South America **27 N4**
P'yongyang *capital city* North Korea **49 P6**
Pyrenees *mountain range* SW Europe **35 P9**

• • Q • •

Qaanaaq Greenland **58 B5**
Qaidam Basin *basin* China **48 I6**
Qaqortoq Greenland **58 A7**
Qarshi Uzbekistan **45 N8**
Qatar *country* SW Asia **43 P7**
Qilian Shan *mountain range* China **48 I6**
Qingdao China **49 O7**
Qiqihar China **49 O4**
Qom Iran **43 P4**
Québec *province capital* Québec, Canada **21 O10**
Québec *province* Canada **21 O8**
Queen Charlotte Islands *island group* Canada **20 F7**
Queen Elizabeth Islands *island group* Canada **20 J3**
Queen Maud Land *physical region* Antarctica **59 Q7**
Queen Maud Mountains *mountain range* Antarctica **59 P9**
Queensland *state* Australia **53 N5**
Queenstown New Zealand **56 H10**
Queretaro Mexico **24 G7**
Quetta Pakistan **47 K3**
Quito *capital city* Ecuador **27 M4**

• • R • •

Rabat *capital city* Morocco **28 H5**
Rach Gia Vietnam **50 I6**
Rajkot India **47 L6**
Rajshahi Bangladesh **47 R5**
Raleigh *state capital* North Carolina, USA **23 R7**
Ralik Chain *island group* Marshall Islands **55 K5**
Ranchi India **47 Q6**
Rangitikei *river* New Zealand **57 M6**
Rarotonga *island* Cook Islands **55 O9**
Rasht Iran **43 P3**
Ratak Chain *island group* Marshall Islands **55 L4**
Rawalpindi Pakistan **47 M2**
Recife Brazil **27 T5**
Red Deer Alberta, Canada **20 H8**
Red River *river* USA **23 M8**
Red Sea *sea* NW Indian Ocean **10 D6**
Regina *province capital* Saskatchewan, Canada **20 J9**
Reims France **35 Q6**
Reindeer Lake *lake* Canada **20 J7**
Rennes France **35 O6**
Réunion *French territory* SW Indian Ocean **31 O9**
Réunion *island* W Indian Ocean **10 E9**
Revillagigedo, Islas *island group* Mexico **24 D7**
Reykjavik *capital city* Iceland **33 L2**
Rhine *river* W Europe **10 C4**
Rhode Island *state* USA **23 S5**
Rhodes *island* Greece **39 Q11**
Rhodope Mountains *mountain range* Bulgaria **39 N8**
Rhône *river* France/Switzerland **35 Q8**
Richmond *state capital* Virginia, USA **23 R6**
Riga *capital city* Latvia **33 Q10**
Riga, Gulf of *sea feature* NE Atlantic Ocean **33 Q9**
Rijeka Croatia **39 K6**
Rio Branco Brazil **27 O5**
Rio de Janeiro Brazil **27 R7**
Riyadh *capital city* Saudi Arabia **43 O8**
Rockhampton Queensland, Australia **53 Q6**
Rocky Mountains *mountain range* Canada/USA **11 O4**
Romania *country* SE Europe **39 O6**
Rome *capital city* Italy **37 N9**
Ronne Ice Shelf *ice shelf* Antarctica **59 O8**
Rosario Argentina **27 P9**
Ross Ice Shelf *ice shelf* Antarctica **59 P10**
Ross Sea *sea* Southern Ocean **59 P11**
Rostov-na-Donu Russia **40 D8**
Rotorua New Zealand **57 M4**
Rotorua, Lake *lake* New Zealand **57 M4**
Rotterdam Netherlands **35 Q4**
Ruapehu, Mount *mountain* New Zealand **57 L5**
Ruse Bulgaria **39 P7**
Russia *country* Asia/Europe **40 I8**
Rwanda *country* C Africa **31 L5**

General index

Picture sources

Picthall and Gunzi would like to thank the following individuals and organisations for their permission to use their photographs:

Abbreviations
t = top; b = bottom; c = centre; r = right; l = left.

Aloysius Han - www.geohavens.com for the rubies on p50; Alstom; Automobili Lamborghini SpA; CN Tower, Canada; Dickinson by Design; Ford Motor Company; International Crane Foundation, Baraboo, Wisconsin; Jumeirah International; Memories of New Zealand - www.memoriesofnz.co.nz; Saab Great Britain Ltd

Ardea: John Wombe/Auscape/ Ardea.com 53 bc

Britain on View: www.britainonview.com 34 bc

Bruce Coleman: 55 cr

Corbis: Tiziana and Gianni Baldizzone: 32 tr; Sharna Balfour; Gallo Images: 31 tr; Tom Bean: 36 bl; Fernando Bengoechea/Beateworks: 35 tr; Tibor Bognar: 46 cl, 46 cl; Christophe Boisvieux: 17 br; Simonpietri Christian/Corbis Sygma: 9 br; Arko Datta/Reuters: 46 cl; Colin Dixon/Arcaid: 38 crb; DLILLC: 30 bc, 56 cr; epa: 14 cl; Alejandro Ernesto/epa: 14 bl; Randy Faris: 24 bl; Paddy Fields -

Louie Psihoyos: 50 bl; Franz Marc Frei: 56 bl; Natalie Fobes: 35 br; Owen Franken: 17 tr; Darrell Gulin: 15 tr; Ainal Abd Halim/Reuters: 42 tr; Lindsay Hebberd: 17 tl; Chris Hellier: 31 cr; Dallas and John Heaton/ Free Agents Limited: 29 br, 49 tr; Jon Hicks: 27 br; Robert van der Hilst: 38 cl; Eric and David Hosking: 15 bcl; Hanan Isachar: 43 tr; Wolfgang Kaehler: 15 tl,15 br, 54 bl; Catherine Karnow: 38 cr, 55 tr; Frank Krahmer/zefa: 27 cl; Jacques Langevin/Corbis Sygma: 41 tr; Danny Lehman: 25 br; John and Lisa Merrill: 36 c; Viviane Moos: 46 tr; Kazuyoshi Nomachi: 29 tc; Neil Rabinowitz: 57 cr; Finbarr O'Reilly/Reuters: 16 tr; José Fuste Raga/zefa: 14 br, 22 bl, 34 cr, 49 br, 50 c; Carmen Redondo: 32 br; Reuters: 26 cr, 53 tr; Guenter Rossenbach/zefa: 15 tcl; Galen Rowell: 55 tl, 58 cr; Anders Ryman: 52 cl; Kevin Schafer: 9 bc; Alfio Scigliano/Sygma/Corbis: 37 br; Paul Seheult/Eye Ubiquitous: 26 tr, Hugh Sitton/zefa: 51 tl; Hubert Stadler: 15 tcr; Paul A. Souders: 33 cr; Jon Sparks: 42 bl; Shannon Stapleton/Reuters: 16 bl; Hans Strand: 56 tr; Staffan Widstrand: 37 cr; Uli Wiesmeier/zefa: 36 tr; Tony Wharton/ Frank Lane Picture Agency: 37 tr; Larry Williams: 25 tr; Valdrin Xhemaj/epa: 21 tc; Shamil Zhumatov/Reuters: 44 c.

ESA: 8 cl, c, cr, 9 cl, c, ca, cr.

FLPA: Ingo Arndt/Foto Natural/Minden Pictures: 38 bc; Richard Becker: 14 tr; Jim Brandenburg/Minden Pictures: 48 cl; Hans Dieter Brandl: 32 cr; Michael Callan: 32 cl; R.Dirscherl: 51 cr;

Gerry Ellis/Minden Pictures: 48 bl; im Fitzharris/Minden Pictures/FLPA: 20 bl; Michael & Patricia Fogden/Minden Pictures: 24 bc; Michael Gore: 52 c; Rev. Bruce Henry: 46 br; Michio Hoshino/Minden Pictures: 23 tr, 58 br; Mitsuaki Iwago /Minden Pictures: 52 bc; Frank W Lane: 45 tr; Frans Lanting: 23 bc, 26 bc, 29 cr; Thomas Mangelsen/Minden Picture: 4-5 b; S & D & K Maslowski: 20 bc; Claus Meyer/Minden Pictures: 26 cl; Yva Momatiuk /John Eastcott/Minden Pictures: 27 tr; Colin Monteath /Minden Pictures: 47 tr; Rinie van Muers/Foto Natura: 3 c, 59 tr; Mark Newman: 41 tl; Flip Nicklin/Minden Picture: 21 tr; R & M Van Nostrand: 28 bl; Alan Parker: 44 bl; Walter Rohdich: 46 cr; L Lee Rue: 21 cr; Cyril Ruoso\JH Editorial/Minden Pictures: 36 br; Silvestris Fotoservice: 39 cr; Jurgen & Christine Sohns: 31 tc, 44 br; Inga Spence: 42 bc; Egmont Strigl/ Imagebroker/FLPA: 45 br; Chris & Tilde Stuart: 43 br; Terry Andrewartha: 58 tr; Barbara Todd/ Hedgehog House/Minden Pictures: 59 cr; Winfried Wisniewski: 40 cl, 59 bl; Terry Whittaker: 34 tr; Konrad Wothe/Minden Pictures: 40 bc; Zhinong Xi/Minden Pictures: 49 tl; Shin Yoshino/Minden Pictures: 53 cr.

Andy Crawford: 51 br

Steve Gorton: 24 c, 34 cl, 36 c, 38 tc, bc, 41 bl, 42 c, 45 tl, cr, 47 cl, bc, 49 cr, 51 c, 54 tr, 54 tr, 54 bc

NASA: 9 tr, 23 br.

Chez Picthall: 2 b, 23 tc, 41 br.

Peter Picthall: 28 cl

Still Pictures: K. Thomas/Still Pictures: 39 tl

Warren Photographic: Jane Burton: 39 br, 50 tr, 57 br; Kim Taylor and Mark Taylor: 32 c; Mark Taylor: 50 tl, Monarch butterflies © Warren Photographic: 24 tc.

Dominic Zwemmer: 14 cl, 15 bc, 30 cl, 53 br, 57 ac

Front cover
Main image: NASA; Tim Graham/Corbis: tl; DLILLC/Corbis: cl; Michael Gore FLPA: clb; Cyril Ruoso\JH Editoria/Minden Pictures/FLPA: bl.

Back cover
Jose Fuste Raga/Corbis: tl, cl; Warren photographic: clb; NASA: bl.

All other images © of Picthall and Gunzi.

Every effort has been made to trace the copyright holders and we apologise in advance for any unintentional omissions. We would be pleased to insert the appropriate acknowledgement in any subsequent edition of this book.

Continents of the world

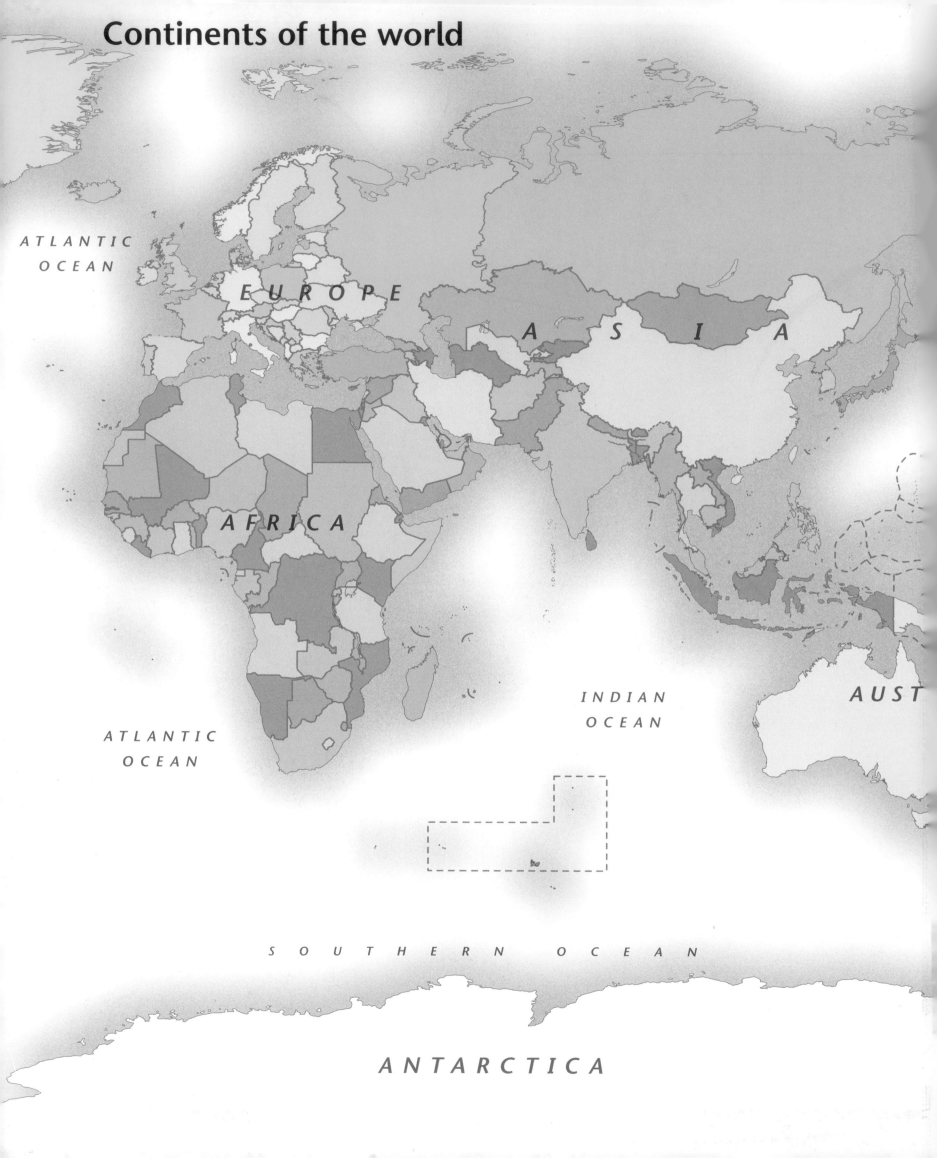